D0923303

ENCINA HIGH SCHOOL
T 12591

HISTORICAL NEEDLEWORK OF PENNSYLVANIA

HISTORICAL

NEEDLEWORK OF PENNSYLVANIA

Margaret B. Schiffer

New York CHARLES SCRIBNER'S SONS

All color photographs and the black and white photograph on page 54 are by Carl W. Bucks; all other photographs, except those credited to various sources on pages 29 (bottom), 41, 59, 65 (top), 68, 95 and 101, are by Ned Goode.

THIS BOOK PUBLISHED SIMULTANEOUSLY IN THE UNITED STATES OF AMERICA AND IN CANADA—COPYRIGHT UNDER THE BERNE CONVENTION

A-7.68 [MC]

PRINTED IN THE UNITED STATES OF AMERICA
Library of Congress Catalog Card Number 68-17348

IN MEMORY OF

Ellen Waln Harrison McMichael

MY GRANDMOTHER

Contents

Acknowledgments

I wish to thank the following collectors, museums and schools for permission to include pictures of their needlework: Annie S. Kemerer Museum, Chester County Historical Society, Cooper Union Museum, Titus C. Geesey, Henry Francis duPont Winterthur Museum, Historical Society of Berks County, Historical Society of York County, Historical Society of Pennsylvania, Johannes Mueller House, Mr. & Mrs. Francis E. Judson, Joe Kindig Jr., Lancaster County Historical Society, Linden Hall School, Mrs. W. Logan MacCoy, Mrs. Richard McIlnay, Mercer Museum of Bucks County Historical Society, Metropolitan Museum of Art, Moravian Museum of Bethlehem, Mr. & Mrs. Samuel W. Morris, Museum of Art Carnegie Institute, Mrs. James Rawle, Mrs. Joseph Russell, Schwenkfelder Library, Schwenkfelder Museum, Mrs. J. Stodgell Stokes, Mrs. Robert Williams Trump, Mrs. J. Ramsey VanRoden, Mr. & Mrs. George Vaux, Westtown School and Whitefield House Museum Moravian Historical Society.

I would also like to thank the following people for their assistance in locating and making possible the photographing of the needlework: Miss Alice B. Beer, Miss Clair Conway, Byron K. Horne, Mrs. Charles Lundgren, David Milgrome, Harry L. Rinker, Mrs. J. Paul Sias, Charles B. Simmons, Mrs. F. P. Stocker, Mrs. Joseph P. Strakey, Rev. Edward H. Swaverly, Mrs. Daniel D. Test Jr., Nicholas B. Wainwright and Mrs. Henry Walter Jr.

My thanks too, to Mrs. Florence M. Montgomery who introduced me to Randle Holmes *The Academy of Armory; or a Display of Heraldry;* to Eric de Jonge, who shared a part of his knowledge of symbolism with me; Frank H. Sommer, who made many books available to me and to Charles F. Montgomery who has been most helpful to me in all my researching projects.

My especial appreciation goes to Bart Anderson and Herbert F. Schiffer who from the beginning have offered encouragement and help with the manuscript, Mrs. Margareta F. Lyons for her work in designing the lay-out of this book, and to Miss Elinor Parker for her interest, advice and assistance throughout the production.

HISTORICAL NEEDLEWORK OF PENNSYLVANIA

INTRODUCTION

IT was William Penn's plan for Pennsylvania that it should be a "Holy Experiment" where men would have the opportunity to make a new start in the world. In 1667 Penn had formally joined the Friends, generally called Quakers, and in 1681 he had written: "After many waitings, watching, soliciting, and disputes in council my country was confirmed to me under the great seal of England. God will bless and make it the seed of a nation." To this territory was given the name of Pennsylvania. A number of settlers, mainly Dutch, Swedes, Finns and English, had been living in the newly formed territory of Pennsylvania for some years among the American Indians.

William Penn, who was a skillful organizer anxious to convert his wilderness into productive land, set about publicizing the advantages of his colony to Englishmen, Germans, Frenchmen and Dutchmen. Through pamphlets and other publications, especially in Germany, the news was quickly circulated that a new land had opened flowing with opportunity and productivity where both political and religious liberty were promised.

Three main motivating forces influenced the different religious, ethnic and national groups that contributed to the settling of Pennsylvania: the desire for religious freedom, relief from political persecution and economic advantages.

The greatest number of settlers to Pennsylvania after 1682 came from the British Isles. It was quite natural that the majority were Quakers. Penn had a concern for the establishing of a haven of refuge for the Friends in the New World. Not all of these were English. The so-called Welsh Barony was settled by Welsh Quakers and Germantown by German Quakers. There were also a few Irish Quakers in the colony. Many Quakers came from other colonies, some from the West Indies and a few from Maryland and Virginia. A number of English Anglicans also settled in Pennsylvania.

The Germans, beginning in 1683, arrived in Pennsylvania by way of Philadelphia. They spread out quickly into the country outside the periphery of early English and Quaker settlements. Germany at this time was a collection of principalities each with its own ruler and a state religion. There was little sympathy for dissenters, and furthermore the entire country was suffering from the ravages of the Thirty Years War. A religious movement known as Pietism had swept Europe. The German sects produced by Pietism had much in common with the Quakers.

The Mennonites were among the first of the sects to come in large numbers. In 1683 they planted the first colony in America in Germantown. Later they settled in Montgomery, Bucks and Lancaster counties. The Moravians founded Bethlehem in 1741. The first substantial Amish colony arrived in Philadelphia in 1737. They later settled along the Northkill Creek in the northwestern part of Berks County, in Lancaster and Mifflin counties. The Brethren or Dunkards settled in Lancaster County. The Schwenkfelders from Silesia settled in upper Montgomery, eastern Berks, upper Bucks and lower Northampton counties.

Later, large numbers of Germans who belonged to the Reformed or Lutheran persuasion settled in Lancaster, Bucks and Berks counties. They were known as Church People. By 1750 Pennsylvania was considered in Germany to be the land of opportunity. The peak of German immigration was reached in 1755.

Since the Germans were predominantly farm folk they sought

fertile farm soils as the place to settle. The so-called Pennsylvania Dutch country of today was the area most heavily populated. The Pennsylvania Germans hung onto their close way of life, their churches and schools which perpetuated their language, culture and manner of living. The Germans had the reputation of being the best farmers in America.

Between 1717 and 1776 a large number of Scotch-Irish Presbyterians arrived in Pennsylvania. They were mostly farmers or men skilled in the manufacture of wool. The English and Germans had taken possession of most of the choice land in eastern Pennsylvania. The Scotch-Irish by 1720 were in central Pennsylvania in upper Lancaster and Dauphin counties and in later years they moved into the Cumberland Valley. A few French Huguenots and Roman Catholics settled within the boundaries.

William Penn's belief in Pennsylvania became a reality. By the time of the American Revolution, in 1775, Philadelphia was the second largest city in the English-speaking world and until about 1840 Pennsylvania was known as the "breadbasket of America."

This combination of opportunity and political and religious freedom to men from various nations unknown in the Old World made Pennsylvania America's first melting pot.

From the time of settlement the Quakers, Moravians and Scotch-Irish believed in education. The Quakers and the Moravians were well ahead of their time in their belief in education for women and Pennsylvania was one of the first colonies to have schools for girls. In colonial Pennsylvania the church and school were often one but there were also neighbourhood schools, dame schools, petty schools, night schools, boarding schools and public schools that girls could attend.

The first Moravian School for girls was started in Germantown in 1742. In Philadelphia girls were admitted to the Friends Public School for elementary subjects and in 1754 Anthony Benezet was able to persuade the overseers to admit them to grammar school. In 1753 William Dawson had opened a night school for working girls and in 1767 Anthony Benezet had started a morning school for poor girls. Embroidery, both plain and ornamental, was part of the curriculum.

Caulfeild and Saward in the *Dictionary of Needlework* define embroidery as "An art which consists of enriching a flat foundation by working into it with a needle coloured silks, gold or silver thread, and other extraneous materials, in floral, geometric, or figure designs. The origin of embroidery is lost in antiquity, but it is known to have existed before painting, and to have been the first medium of reproducing natural objects in their natural colour. The work came from the East, and was first called Phrygium, or Phrygian work, while an embroiderer was called Phrygio. . ."

A great deal of the early surviving Pennsylvania needlework stems from the needlework of Great Britain, but because of the restrictions of materials and limited time of the Colonial women they did not indulge in the more elaborate designs. The Quakers believed that their clothing and the furnishings of their homes should be "of the best sort but plain." Samplers, canvas work, crewel work and silk embroidery have survived made by girls of English descent during the eighteenth century.

The so-called Pennsylvania Dutch insisted for more than a century on the maintenance of their own church schools conducted in the German language, which made Pennsylvania bilingual. Since they were mostly farmers the Pennsylvania Dutch tended to regard education as of doubtful value beyond reading, writing and simple arithmetic. The girls were taught, however, the traditional German patterns and designs on samplers that would later be used on show towels, tablecloths and other linens. The Pennsylvania German samplers are more truly samplers with their lack of arrangement than those worked by the English girls or girls of English descent. The Pennsylvania Germans had an instinctive love of color. Examples of their needlework dating before 1800 are extremely rare.

The Moravians were particularly known in Pennsylvania for their love of music, missionary work and for their excellent schools. The Sisters taught girls both plain and ornamental sewing. In the nineteenth century various types of floral embroidery in colored silks, ribbon and crêpe work in addition to pictorial embroidery in silk became known as Bethlehem or Moravian embroidery. The influence of the Moravian teaching spanned a long enough period of time that a fine standard of embroidery was established in Pennsylvania. Bethlehem was one of the major sources of the most skillful needlework art in America.

The ever-recurring designs found on Pennsylvania needlework can be traced back to the dim ages of pre-history and are familiar to the student of ancient mythologies. The paired birds and animals (equivalent to the Ying versus Yang of the Chinese), the Tree of Life, the Sun Wheel, the Stars and even the wavy border lines were part and parcel of ancient symbols and symbolism of the past.

The pairs of birds or animals, sometimes facing one another and sometimes opposed, symbolize good and evil, day and night, summer and winter, et cetera. The Tree of Life in all its forms is of very ancient origin. The branches when raised symbolize new life sprouting, and when drooping life extinguishing. In some instances some branches are raised while others droop, symbolizing that as life is dying a new life is beginning, the never-ending process of nature and of man. The Tree of Life can be shown growing from the earth but frequently a basket or urn is embroidered instead to represent the mother earth.

The variations of the wavy or zigzag lines, frequently used as borders on samplers, symbolized day and night, the changing seasons and flowing water. Adam and Eve symbolize good and evil. In a few instances Adam and Eve and paired birds or animals are found. The sun wheel and star motifs date back to prehistoric days when people were more superstitious and worshiped more than one God. The oak leaf is a sign of strength.

The symbolism of flowers has been cultivated in all lands. The tulip was brought from the East to the West during the sixteenth century. It is frequently interpreted as the symbol of the Trinity. The rose is the flower that has the greatest prominence in the mythology of the West. It is the symbol of all flowers and of beauty. In Pennsylvania needlework the carnation was often embroidered. It reached England from India and Persia.

Colors were symbolically used from the earliest time. White was the emblem of purity, virginity, innocence, faith, life, joy and light; red represents suffering and martyrdom; the passion of our Lord; it also signifies divine love, power, blood, war and anguish; blue is emblematic of piety, sincerity, godliness, fidelity; yellow and gold, the goodness of God, faith, faithfulness; green, emblem of hope, joy, mirth, youth, bountifulness and prosperity; violet, passion, suffering, sorrow, humility, love and truth, and black the symbolic color of death, darkness, despair, sorrow, mourning and deep humiliation.

There are many more recurrent symbols but the above-mentioned motifs are those most frequently encountered in Pennsylvania needlework.

1781 sampler of Susanna Head, of Philadelphia. Embroidered in silk, on linen, using petit point, satin, French knot, cross, eyelet and brick stitches. A bead is used for the eye of each bird. $12\frac{3}{4}'' \times 18\frac{3}{4}''$. MR. & MRS. GEORGE VAUX.

PLATE I

SAMPLERS

PENNSYLVANIA eighteenth and nineteenth century samplers have long been treasured by the families of the makers, collectors of needlework, and museums. The majority of the samplers were worked in silk on linen by young girls. The designs were seldom original with the worker; instead, the motifs had been handed down from mother to daughter or teacher to pupil through the generations. The patterns were usually drawn directly on the linen with pen or pencil.

The commonest samplers found contain merely the alphabet, or alphabets and numerals. Others have wonderful mixtures of animals, birds, trees, urns, houses, baskets of flowers and fruit, et cetera. Some Pennsylvania samplers include initials of members of the family and friends while other samplers were Family Records which listed the names of parents, brothers and sisters.

A few of the Pennsylvania samplers have human figures with faces and hands painted on the ground and others have faces painted on paper that were attached to the ground. On a few of the more elaborate Pennsylvania samplers sequins and metallic threads were used in addition to silk thread.

Sampler derived from the Latin *exemplar* is defined by Palsgrave [ed. 1530] as "an exampler for a woman to work by"; by Bailey [ed. 1735] as "[exemplar] a Pattern or Model; also a Piece of Work by young Girls for Improvement"; by Webster [ed. 1828] as "A pattern of work; particularly, a piece of needlework by young girls for improvement"; and by Caulfeild and Saward's *Dictionary of Needlework* as "Samplers, or, as they were first called, Sam Cloths, first came into use during the sixteenth century, on account of the great scarcity and high price of Lace pattern books; therefore, all the earliest laces, such as Cut Works, Drawn Threads, Reticellas, et cetera, were copied upon Sam Cloths by those who were not sufficiently rich to buy the pattern books, with the combined purpose of obtaining the design, and exhibiting the proficiency of the worker. At a later date, when lace was not so much made, and designs of all kinds were more abundant, Samplers were still worked, no longer with the object of perpetuating a pattern, but to exhibit the skill of the embroiderer; and no young lady's education, during the seventeenth and eighteenth centuries, was considered complete until she had embroidered in silks and gold thread a Sampler with a bordering of Drawn Work, and a centre filled with representations of animals, flowers, and trees, accompanied by verses appropriate to the undertaking. These Samplers were looked upon as such proofs of skill that they were preserved with much care . . ."

American seventeenth century samplers were long and narrow. The upper section usually had band designs in color of conventionalized strawberries, tulips, roses, trefoil, Indian pink, the Tree of Life and geometric designs, used either alone or in combination. Infrequently a human figure or an alphabet was included. The lower half was often filled with drawn or cut work designs embroidered completely in white. The early samplers, worked on linen, rarely had names and dates. They may well have been worked over a period of time, for practical purposes and as a means of recording patterns for future use by girls and women. The needlework on the earlier samplers is generally far superior to that found on later examples.

No dated seventeenth century Pennsylvania sampler is known to have survived. The sampler, worked by Hester Beale, an English Quaker, born in Chester County in 1701, has many of the early features. [p.23] It is long and narrow, embroidered completely, using cross border or band patterns and has no name or date. Green, blue and yellow silk are embroidered on the linen ground using the back stitch.

1727 sampler by Mary Morris of Philadelphia. Embroidered in silk on linen using cross, satin, long and short, eyelet, stem, French knot and queen stitches. The colors used are yellow, blue, green, brown, purple and pink. $14\frac{1}{2}'' \times 11\frac{1}{2}''$. MRS. JAMES RAWLE.

The earliest dated Pennsylvania sampler found thus far is that made by Susanna Painter, of Philadelphia, in 1724, at the age of seven years.[1] Using eyelet and cross stitches she embroidered two alphabets and an inscription: "The blessing of the Lord: it maketh rich and he addeth no sorrow with it."

Three years later, in 1727, Mary Morris and Ann Marsh[2] made very similar band type samplers. Mary Morris was the daughter of Anthony Morris 2nd, and wife of Samuel Powel 2nd, of Philadelphia. Ann Marsh was an English girl, who came to Philadelphia and taught in a Friends school there. In both samplers there are two lines of verse or a prose quotation of a religious nature with rather elaborate cross borders, some of which return to seventeenth century designs; then two more lines of verse or prose and another border, and so on until near the bottom of the sampler names of members of the families are listed. Mary Morris stitched the following sentiments:

> Men Fearing God Are Oft Exposed We see To Various Temptations and Calamitie. Twas Joseph's Lot To Meet Many Crosses
> But God At Last Did Recompense His Losses. What Man Designs For Ill
> God Changes And Turns It To Good By His Almighty Hand.

> the bed was earth the raised pillow stone wheron poor Jacob rest his head his home heaven and his canopie the shades of night,
> Where no drawn curtains to exclude the light poor state of Jacob here it seems so at his cradle found, as soft a bed as he.

> Lord Give Me Wisdom To Direct My Ways I Ask Not Riches Nor Yet Length Of Days
> My Life's A Flower The Time Is Morn To Last Is Mixt, With Frost And Snow With Every Blast.

> oh thou great king of kings arise and reign except thy virtue spring all worships vain
> except thy quickening power be felt to rise theirs none can offer us a sacrifice.

That Finds Acceptance, With So Great A King And Then Who Dare Into Thy Presence Bring
The Blemished The Maimed Or The Blind Which With An Earthly Prince Could Never Find.

any regard but rather for the same severe chastisement with rebuke and shame o let thy holy power operate
within thy temple thou immaculate holy high priest o let thy hand prepare the sacrifice then Israel may not fear

To Find Admittance To The Royal Throne Thou'll Smell Sweetness And Accept Thy Own
We'll Wait In Patience And Depend On Thee Thou Only Canst Rebuke The Enemy

Twenty-seven names are listed and then she embroidered: "this work in hand my friends may have when I am dead and laid in grave Mary Morris her work in y[e] year 1727." [p. 19]

Both samplers have conventionalized flower borders and the stitches used are more varied than will be found in samplers of a later date. Acorns, roses, strawberries, carnations and pine trees are included in the design. In this period American samplers were becoming shorter and broader and almost always included a border design, name and date.

In 1744 Mary Keasley embroidered a sampler very similar to those of Mary Morris and Ann Marsh.[3]

In 1728 a boarding school was advertised in Philadelphia:

> A Boarding School, also Reading, Writing, Cyphering, Dancing, and several sorts of Needle-work, at the House of George Brownell, in Second-Street, Philadelphia.[4]

When Anthony Benezet first began teaching in the Girls' School, in Philadelphia in 1754, he was required to teach reading, writing, arithmetic, and English grammar. Such schools were known as English schools. In addition to these English schools there were "petty schools" such as those kept by Debby Godfrey, who taught some poor children to sew and read, and another taught by Ann Redman in 1761 which had previously been taught by Rebeckah Burchall, where the girls were taught reading, writing and plain sewing.[5]

In the last third of the eighteenth century the records of the monthly meetings of Philadelphia, Horsham, Darby and others, indicate that the curriculum consisted of reading, English, writing, mathematics, sewing, spelling, needlework, and other subjects suitable for girls.[6] In 1799 Mrs. Clarke taught boys and girls reading and she also taught sewing to the girls. Ann Marsh, who was previously mentioned, had a school similar to that of Mrs. Clarke's.[7]

In mid-eighteenth century a distinctive type of sampler began to be embroidered in Pennsylvania. Around the edges are conventionalized floral borders while the center is divided into squares in which floral motifs and verses are worked in alternating squares. From this period on, pious verses were extremely popular and are frequently found on samplers.

In 1753 Ann Flower, daughter of Enoch Flower, who was one of the early schoolteachers in Pennsylvania, started a sampler.[8] The border has diagonal lines and a few strawberries and leaves. Below the border is inscribed: "Lord Give Me Wisdom To Direct My Ways I bre Not Riches Nor Yet Lerneth of Days Ann Flowe." The center section has been divided into nine squares in one of which is marked: "Oh if my mind should be inclin d." At the bottom of the center section is wrought: "Ann Flower Her Work Made In The Year 1753." The sampler is embroidered in silk on a linen ground using eyelet, satin and petit point stitches in green, blue, gold, pink and black.

Mary Webb, of York, worked this type of sampler in 1760 using tent, satin and cross stitches. The border has zigzag lines, carnations and vines with a tulip in each corner.[9] The inner border has a chain design. The center section is divided into nine squares with sprays of different flowers in the center and four corners and the following verses in the remaining four squares.

Let us my Friend all peevish self withstand
And in the meekness of the spotless lamb
Lead one another gently by the Hand

And travel forward to the Holy Land,
Where the Redeemed on Mount Zion stand,
With Harps of living praises in their Hands

Oh if My Mind
Should be inclined
This would increase my fear
Lord from above
Thou God of love
Reveal thy counsel near

That I may know
That I may do
Thy ever blessed will
Ah! thine alone
And not mine own
Great King! do thou fulfil

One look of mercy from thy eye
One whisper of thy voice
Exceed a whole eternity
Employ'd in carnal joys

Could I the spacious earth command
Or move the boundless sea
For one dear hour at thy right hand
I'd give them both away.

Consider well some my past days
On former Times reflect
And see if thou in all thy ways
Are truly Circumspect.

Joseph Webb Edith Webb H W
Mary Webb Her Work In the
Thirteenth Year of her age 1766

Early type sampler by Hester Beale born in Chester County in 1701. Embroidered in silk on linen using the back stitch. The colors used are green, blue and yellow. 23″ × 9½″. CHESTER COUNTY HISTORICAL SOCIETY.

In 1781 Susanna Head, of Philadelphia, at the age of fifteen embroidered a sampler which she divided into twelve squares. [plate I] Alternating squares have pious sentiments and sprays of different flowers. Four of the groups of flowers have birds with bead eyes. Around the border are the same zigzag lines used by Mary Morris, Ann Flower and Mary Webb. Susanna Head also worked floral motifs and strawberries between the diagonal lines. This sampler is well executed, using tent, satin, cross, eyelet, brick and French knots in silk on a linen ground. The sampler is surprisingly colorful. Many of the eighteenth century samplers are so faded that it is difficult today to be certain of the original colors.

The earliest Pennsylvania school sampler, found thus far, is that made by Lydia Hoopes, in 1765, in the tenth year of her age, at Mrs. Hollis's School, in Goshen Township, Chester County. [p. 25]

> The girls were taught by Mistress Hollis, who conducted a small school in her own residence, about a mile from their home. She enforced habits of strict obedience and attention, regulated their manners, and required an erect posture in their exercises. Punctuality was exacted while under her care; although their path homeward led through their father's orchard where tempting fruits often lay on the ground, they were expected to walk straight to their own door, enter, and hang up their bonnets before they were at liberty to touch apple, plum or pear.
>
> Probably their literary advantages were few compared with those now enjoyed by young ladies, but the result was a facility for action in every department of woman's life and the art of producing an extraordinary amount of fine needlework. I remember many specimens of my grandmother's skill and dexterity, and so clear was her eyesight that she could embroider by moonlight.[10]

RIGHT. 1765 sampler of Lydia Hoopes worked at Mrs. Hollis's School. Goshen Township, Chester County. Embroidered in wool on linen using cross and eyelet stitches. The colors used are green, blue, yellow and purple. 16″ × 10″. MRS. JOSEPH RUSSELL.

This sampler, worked in cross and eyelet stitches, includes sets of alphabets, numerals from one to twenty-four, which is unusual, and floral motifs. It also mentions her father and mother, the initials of her brothers and sisters and that it was wrought at "Hollis School MRS in Goshen" and these verses:

[S]arve [t]hy [C]reator
[In] [t]hy [Y]outh
[T]ake [f]or [t]hy [g]uide
[t]he [B]lessed [t]ruth

As is frequently found on the earlier surviving samplers the shades of green, blue, yellow and purple are bright. The letters and numerals learned from working samplers would, in later years, be useful to the girls when marking and listing linens with initials and numbers.

The Dictionary of Needlework by Caulfeild and Saward has this to say about Dresden Point: "The exact date of the introduction of lace making into Germany is still a matter of dispute . . . Dresden became celebrated during the last part of the seventeenth century, and for the whole of the eighteenth, not for a Pillow lace, but for a Drawn lace, an imitation of the Italian Punto Tirato, in which a piece of linen was converted into lace by some of its threads being drawn away, some retained to form a pattern, and others worked together to form square meshes. This Dresden Point was likewise embroidered with fine stitchery . . ." Dresden-type samplers were embroidered, in the Philadelphia area, during the latter half of the eighteenth century. A Dresden sampler was worked on a linen or cotton ground. Sections of the ground were cut out and filled in with needle-made lace, using the buttonhole or hollie point stitch. Hollie point is a twisted buttonhole stitch much used in Church work of the religious houses during the Middle Ages. It was also known as nun's stitch. In the more elaborate Dresden samplers hollie point lace, drawn work and darned lace are combined and worked in linen thread. In addition to the cut and drawn work some samplers also have embroidery in colored silk.

On June 24, 1762 the *Pennsylvania Gazette,* Philadelphia, mentions:

> To be Opened, on the first of July, by
> ELIZABETH SCHARIBROCK,
>
> In third street, between Race and Arch-streets, A SCHOOL for teaching all Manner of Berlin or Dresden NEEDLE-WORK, in the genteelest and most elegant Manner. The Price is Seven Pistoles to learn the whole. Ladies under 12 Years of Age, taken for Ten Shillings Entrance, and Thirty Shillings a Quarter. Attendance will be given them from Ten to Twelve in the Forenoon; and those that it does not suit, from Two to Four in the Afternoon.
> N. B. All Manner of Dresden Work made at the same Place.

The all-white Dresden sampler of Martha Jefferis, of Chester County, is dated 1768. [p. 28] Having the girl's initials and date worked in the hollie point lace, as here, is extremely rare. This sampler has six circles and three rectangles cut from the linen ground, and these spaces are filled with hollie point to form the lace patterns. The majority of the Dresden samplers observed have a series of buttonhole stitches surrounding the cut-outs.

The 1784 embroidery of R. Hughes, of Montgomery County, is also a white sampler. [p. 29] It has four cut-out circles, one in each corner, filled with needle-made lace. In the center is a basket of flowers. The flowers, leaves and basket were worked in darned lace. The latter necessitated the removal of certain weft or warp threads of the material and adding decorative stitchery upon the remaining threads. In outlining the flowers and leaves both buttonhole and chain stitches were used. The stems of the flowers and leaves were worked in chain and stem stitches, the veins of some of the leaves being embroidered in back stitch. The buds were wrought in buttonhole stitch and in outlining the basket fine rows of chain stitches have been employed.

1768 Dresden type sampler by Martha Jefferis of Chester County. An all white linen sampler. 11″ × 9½″. CHESTER COUNTY HISTORICAL SOCIETY.

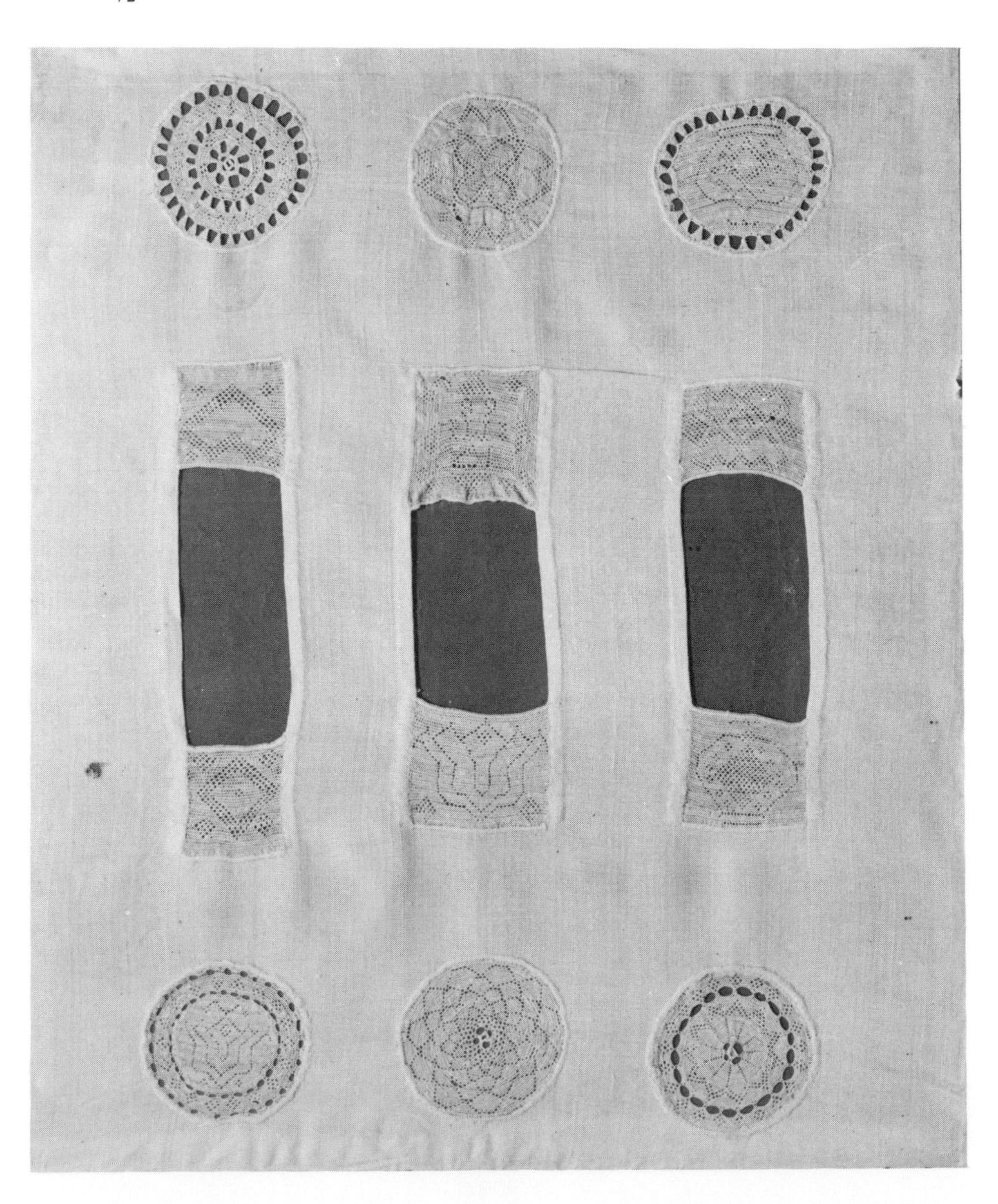

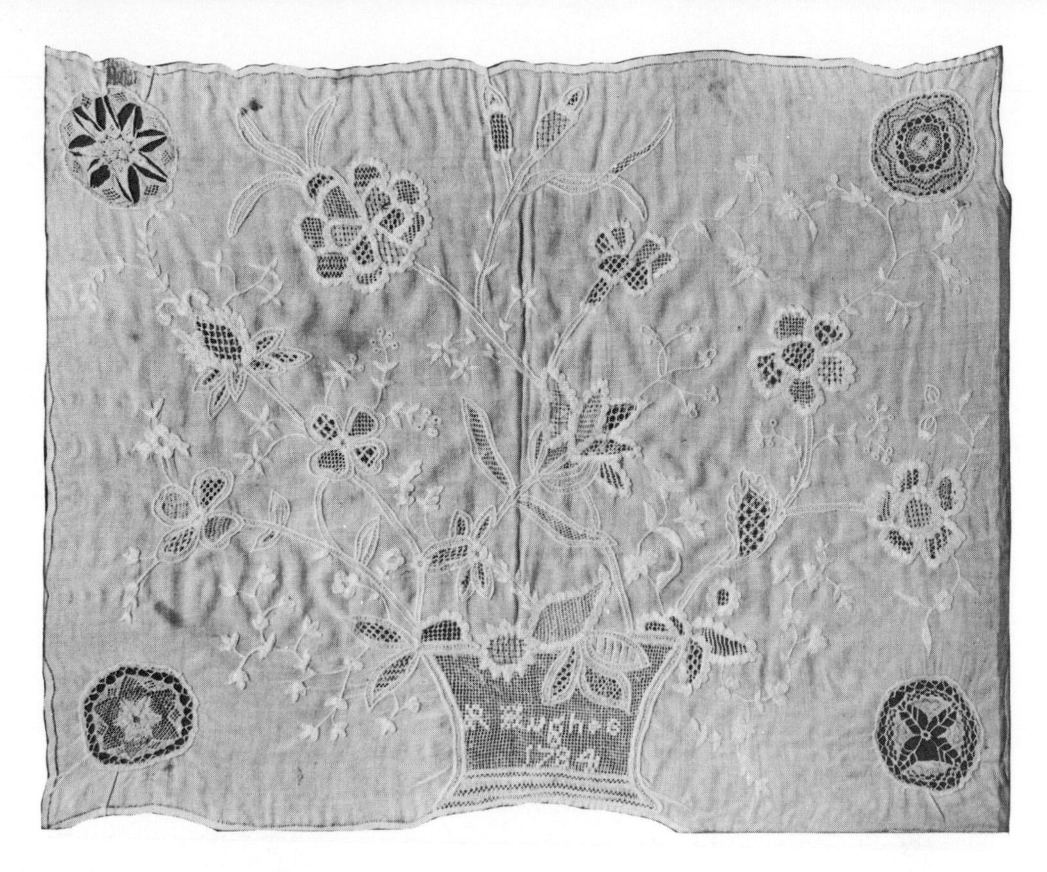

1784 Dresden type and Drawn work sampler by R. Hughes of Montgomery County. An all white linen sampler. Chain, stem, satin, back and buttonhole stitches are used. 15″ × 11½″. MRS. W. LOGAN MacCOY.

1788 Dresden type and Drawn work sampler by Frances Paschal, of Darby Township, Delaware County. An all white sampler on cotton. Silk was used for some of the embroidery. Around the border is a pleated green silk ribbon. 8⅞″ × 6″. COURTESY HENRY FRANCIS DUPONT WINTERTHUR MUSEUM; GIFT OF MR. & MRS. DAVIS L. LEWIS, JR.

The 1786 sampler of Elizabeth Yeatman, of Chester County, is the most usual type of Dresden sampler found in Pennsylvania. [p. 31] It has five cut-out circles, filled with hollie point. The border, birds and sprays were embroidered in colored silks.

The 1788 sampler of Frances Paschal, of Darby Township, Chester County, is an all-white sampler with four cut-out circles and with a basket of flowers embroidered in the center. [p. 29] The name of the girl was worked in the rectangular section of the hollie point. An unusual feature found in this sampler is the use of white silk thread for part of the hollie point. As in the R. Hughes' sampler, hollie point has been combined with drawn lace. Around the border is a pleated green silk ribbon.

The most elaborate sampler is that initialed and dated "I G 1790." [p. 31] The five cut-out circles and basket of flowers were worked in hollie point and drawn lace. Surrounding the circles and basket of flowers are flowering vines and birds wrought in gaily colored silks. It is interesting to notice that each cut-out has been filled with a different pattern of hollie point lace.

In 1775 Martha Thomas worked two alphabets in cross and eyelet stitches divided by simple cross borders, a few scattered strawberries and a conventionalized strawberry border. [p. 32] What is unusual are the initials M T and the date 1786 inlaid in the crest of the frame. This is the only frame known that is initialed and dated. The 1796 cross stitch sampler of Ann Wickersham has three alphabets, numerals from one to six, verses, a vase of flowers and again a conventionalized strawberry border. [p. 32] The frame is original and of a rare type.

The mottoes and prayers embroidered by the girls were intended to inculcate good morals and virtue in their youthful minds while they were learning the useful art of needlework. Margaret Hollingsworth, of Montgomery County, in 1785 worked a sampler with a border closely resembling that of Susanna Head. The earlier

1786 Dresden type sampler of Elizabeth Yeatman of Delaware County. Embroidered in silk and cotton on cotton using satin, cross, stem and buttonhole stitches. The colors used are green and yellow. 9½″ × 9″.
THE AUTHOR.

1790 Dresden type and Drawn work sampler. Embroidered in silk and cotton on linen using buttonhole, cross, satin, chain and stem stitches. The colors used are green, blue, pink, yellow, tan, brown and black. 14½″ × 9½.
CHESTER COUNTY HISTORICAL SOCIETY.

borders wrought in cross stitch follow the angular lines made necessary by the stitch itself. Later, when satin and stem stitches were used, the less stiff vines and flowers were possible to embroider. In the center section she worked a prayer and cross borders of roses, acorns and strawberries. It is a very colorful sampler. The capital letters of the prayer have been embroidered in gold and the small letters in brown while the name and date have red capitals and green small letters. The sampler is worked in silk on linen using cross, satin, long and short and stem stitches. [p. 33]

The darning sampler initialed and dated "H C H 1790" was worked in red and blue threads on a linen ground. Although Germany is credited with the earliest darning samplers, similar work was common in Holland and Denmark. They were worked in England near the end of the eighteenth century. Both sides of the material are alike. The linen was cut away and the spaces made filled with the darning patterns in stripe, herringbone and other designs. Pattern darning was a separate subject in the study of needlework and required a high technical skill that would later be used in the repairing of woven textiles. [p. 34]

Hannah Fletcher's 1793 sampler, worked in cross stitch in silk on a linen ground, is an ambitious work for a young girl. At

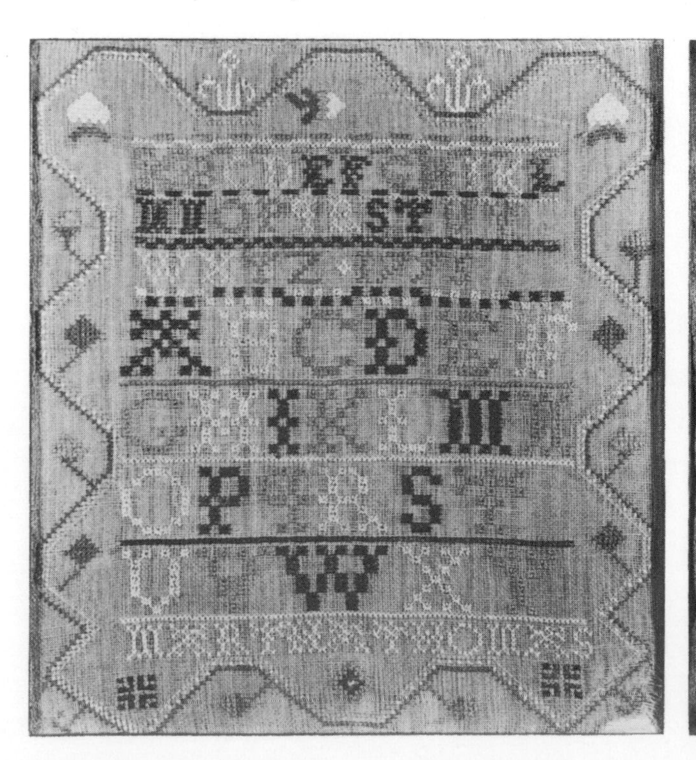

1775 sampler by Martha Thomas. Embroidered in silk on linen using cross, satin and eyelet stitches. The colors used are green, tan, red, black and white. The frame is inlaid "1786 M T". 10½″ × 9½″.
MR. & MRS. FRANCIS E. JUDSON.

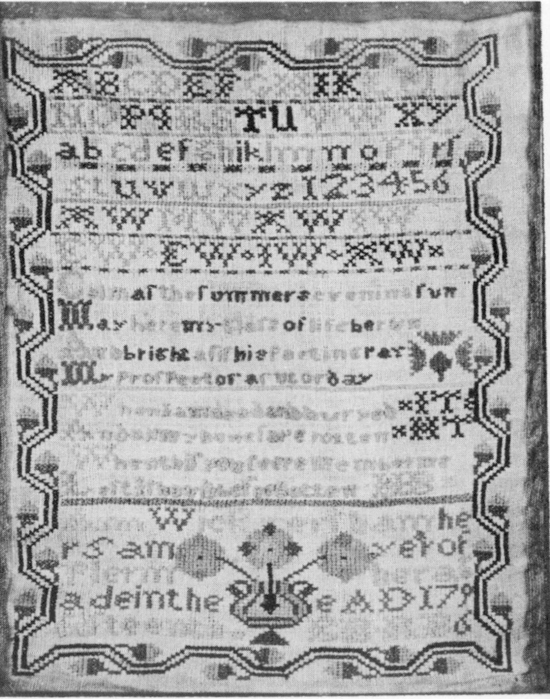

1796 sampler by Ann Wickersham of Chester County. Embroidered in wool on linen in cross stitch. The colors used are green, yellow, brown and black. 9″ × 11″.
THE AUTHOR.

1785 sampler by Margaret Hollingsworth of Montgomery County. Embroidered in silk on linen using cross, satin, long and short and stem stitches. The colors used are red, yellow, gold, cream, blue and gray. 15½″ × 14½″. MRS. W. LOGAN MACCOY.

the top she has mentioned her father and mother, Robert and Priscilla Fletcher, and has embroidered the following verses:

> Indulgent God whos bounteous Care
> Oer all thy worke is shown
> Oh let my grateful praise and prayer
> Ascend before thy throne

1790 darning sampler marked "H C H 1790". Worked on linen. The initials and date in cross stitch. The colors used are red and blue. 11″ × 9″. MRS. MARY ANN McILNAY.

There are balanced strawberry plants in vases, stars, hearts, birds and fruiting trees in the top half of the sampler. At the bottom, on the left, there is a farm house, a picket fence, a procession of ducks on the lawn, a fruiting tree and a pump. In the sky overhead birds are flying. On the right Adam and Eve under a tree are surrounded by two animals, a combination of a dog and a lion. The top half of the sampler is divided from the bottom half in a unique manner: a series of arches have been worked and under each arch there is terra firma and trees. Scattered throughout the sampler initials have been worked, the whole being enclosed by a conventionalized carnation border. [p. 36]

The including of initials on Pennsylvania samplers seems to have been extremely popular. They usually were the initials of members of the family or school friends.

The 1794 sampler of Regina Huebner, a girl of German descent, is a more true sampler in the original meaning of the word. [p. 37] On it she embroidered alphabets, her name, the date and many spot motifs such as crowns, dogs, birds, roosters, baskets and vases of flowers, a castle, a stylized coach pulled by four horses with a driver and two passengers, a key, a chair, a bed, a table, a deer, a heraldic lion and a possible Adam and Eve under a tree growing in a basket over which two birds are flying. Regina Huebner never repeated a motif. The designs, embroidered in silk on a linen ground using cross, chain, eyelet, satin and stem stitches, are not balanced. The embroidery is a record, not a picture, of spot motifs and border designs for later use.

In 1796 a sampler was worked by Peggy Douglass, at Mme. Capron's School in Philadelphia, using stem, satin and cross stitches.[11] She embroidered three alphabets and a strawberry wreath at the bottom enclosing verses. The border included roses, carnations and white berry sprays. Samplers including from one to four alphabets, some numerals and verses, and the girl's name and date continue well into the nineteenth century.

Hannah Brown, of Lancaster, informed "the public and her friends" by advertisement September 3, 1796 that she "had opened a school in Queen Street, opposite to Esquire Graeff's" for the instruction of young ladies in reading, plain sewing, marking, and the different kinds of needlework.[12] From this date until about 1875 many new schools started in the Lancaster area. As life became easier, there was a need and a desire to educate the young girls.

By the 1790's country scenes including houses, shepherds, shepherdesses, flocks of sheep and sometimes other animals and farm buildings were becoming popular subjects for needlework. At this period crinkled silk, most commonly applied in long stitches as a background, began to be employed. Human figures, animals and flowers in the foreground were frequently embroidered in an uncrinkled silk, using satin stitch.

Elizabeth Helms marked her sampler: "Elizabeth Helms Work Done In the 13th Year of her Age Philadelphia April 13th 1798."

1793 sampler by Hannah Fletcher of Germantown. Embroidered in silk on linen in cross stitch. The colors used are red, pink, tan, blue, green, yellow, brown, black and white. 14″ × 17½″. MRS. ROBERT WILLIAMS TRUMP.

[p. 38] The two-story house may well have been her own. There are both post and rail and picket fences. On the lawn an elaborately dressed man and woman walk under the weeping willow trees while in the foreground there is a shepherd, a shepherdess, four sheep, two dogs and one tremendous deer. In the sky flocks of birds are flying. Elizabeth Helms' sense of proportion may have been lacking when

1794 sampler by Regina Huebner, a girl of German descent. Embroidered in silk on linen using eyelet, cross, chain, satin and stem stitches. The colors used are blue, gold, yellow, green and black. 18″ × 23½″. SCHWENKFELDER MUSEUM.

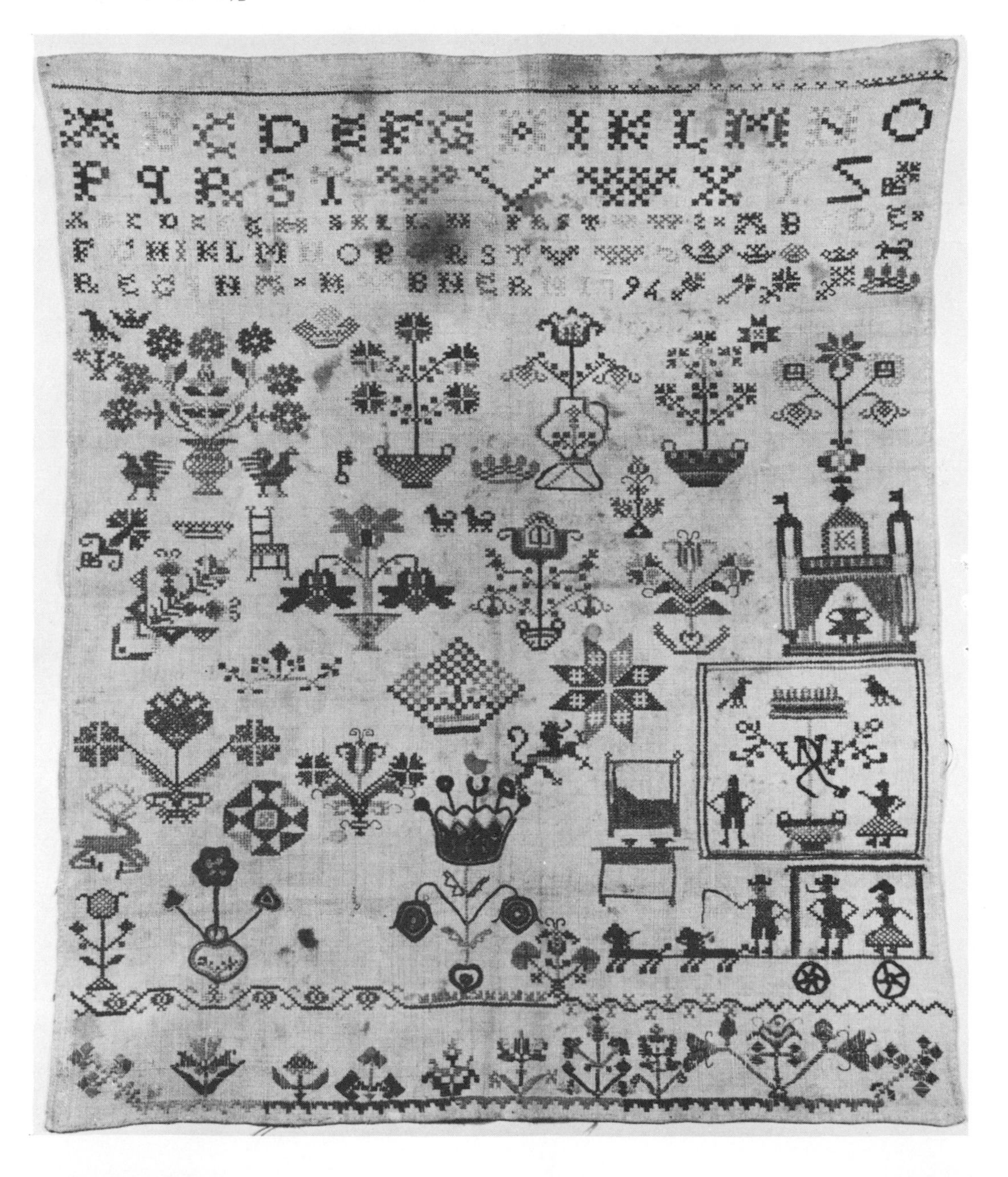

she embroidered the man and woman in the background far larger than the shepherd and shepherdess in the foreground, but the whole country scene is one of charm. Surrounding the sampler is a flower and chain border design.

Architectural samplers were very popular in Pennsylvania. During the 1790's houses began to appear either as a spot motif as found in Hannah Fletcher's 1793 sampler, or as an intrinsical part of the picture as found in Elizabeth Helms' 1798 sampler. In 1799 Sarah Holsworth embroidered one of the most interesting and unusual

1798 sampler by Elizabeth Helms of Philadelphia. Embroidered in silk on linen using cross, tent and an irregularly worked long stitch. The colors used are green, blue, yellow, brown and white. 20″ × 19″. THE AUTHOR.

Pennsylvania samplers. [p. 41] In the center she worked in cross stitch the following:

> Leah Galligher and Rachel Armstrong the Daughters
> of George and Sarah Bratten Was born at one
> birth near Wilmington new Castle County State of
> DelaWare on the 23 day of May and Was bap
> tised in Wilmington Church by the Rev'd Mr.
> Moorman Anno Domini 1764 and Leah Bratten
> Was Married to Francis Galligher by the Rev'd Mr. SteVonson on the 10
> day
> of NoVember 1791
> and Rachel Bratten Was Married to William
> Armstrong September 17 1793 by the same
> Parson SteVonson L G opened School in Lancaster
> on the first Day of May 1797 and had this
> Sampler made by one of her scholars Viz Sarah
> HolsWorth in the year of our LORD 1799
> Dear SaViour take the Children's Hearts and shoot
> thy LoVe's so fastning darts out of thy Heart
> into them all that they May Love thee great and
> small. Think on the tears thy SerVant shed be
> fore this School of babes We had the tears Which
> still do freely run bring to the end What thoust
> begun Lancaster poorhouse

The Lancaster County Poorhouse commenced operations in 1800 following passage of an Act of Legislature entitled "An Act to provide for the erection of Houses of Employment and Support of the Poor in the Counties of Chester and Lancaster." The first building erected to be used for this purpose was not completed until 1801. The building worked by Sarah Holsworth must have been an imaginary one. The birds on the roof and sitting on top of the trees are similar to those used by Sarah N. Barton when she embroidered a picture of Westtown School. [p. 52]

This is the only sampler found, thus far, that mentions not only the names of parents but also that the two sisters were twins, where they were born, baptized, married and by whom and that one sister had opened a school. In 1797 the following advertisement appeared in a Lancaster newspaper:

> MRS. GALLIGHER respectfully informs the inhabitants of this Borough, that she will attend to the instruction of Young Girls: to teach them spelling & reading, also all kinds of plain sewing, knitting and Working of Lace if required. She intends commencing the first day of May next, and will attend from 9 till 12 in the morning and from 2 till 5 in the evening at Mr. Reichenbach's house.[13]

In 1799 a Francis Galligher informed the citizenry through a newspaper advertisement that "he intends opening school on his own account, on Wednesday the 9th inst. in the same house where he taught these preceding two years and a half, and not being any longer subject to the restraint of trustees, in regard of female education."[14]

Sarah Holsworth embroidered the sampler in silk on linen using tent, cross, satin, back, chain, stem, plait, interlaced, braid, eye, rococo, basket and oblong cross stitch in shades of rose, green, blue and cream. Three sides of the border are made up of series of squares containing conventionalized strawberries, hearts, vines, trees and baskets of fruit. At the bottom is the Lancaster Poorhouse, clipped trees, plants growing in urns, birds perched on the Poorhouse and on the trees and strawberries. A number of churches have been found on samplers but this is the only known Pennsylvania public building.

In 1807 Elizabeth Finney in Harrisburg wrought a sampler similar to that worked by Sarah Holsworth in Lancaster, eight years earlier. [plate II] The 1807 sampler is inscribed: "Elizabeth Finney a Daughter of Samuel and Anne Finney was born in Hanover Dauphin County September 11 in the year of our Lord 1791 and made this

Sampler in Harrisburg in Mrs. Leah Meguier's School in the year of our Lord 1807." This Leah Meguier is very probably the Leah Gal-ligher who had a school in Lancaster previously mentioned. The out-side border is divided into squares in which stars, acorns, hearts, birds, baskets of fruit, sprays of flowers and trees in urns with small birds perched on top were embroidered. The inside border had flowers and leaves. The picture in the center shows a man and woman courting and another woman holding a garland of flowers with a basket at

1799 sampler by Sara Holsworth worked at Leah Galligher's School in Lancaster. The build-ing is the Lancaster Poorhouse. Embroidered in silk on linen using tent, satin, cross, back, chain, stem, plait, interlaced braid, eye, rococo, basket and oblong cross stitches. The colors used are rose, green, blue and cream. 17″ × 16½″. COURTESY HENRY FRANCIS DUPONT WINTERTHUR MUSEUM.

her feet, sitting under a willow tree. Sequins decorate the man's coat, the woman's shoes, and form pins on the women's dresses. Purl was used around the head and neck of the seated women and also forms a band on the gentleman's hat. The faces are delicately painted on the ground. Around the border of the sampler is a burnt orange ribbon over which gold edging has been sewn. This is the most elaborate sampler that has been found in Pennsylvania.

In 1825 Ann E. Kelly worked a sampler at Mrs. Meguier's School in Harrisburg using chain, buttonhole, satin and cross stitches.[15] The border is similar to Elizabeth Finney's sampler and is made up of a series of squares containing different designs such as birds, sheep, sprays of flowers, strawberries, basket of fruit, sprays of wheat, a house, tree and fence. In the center, a woman with a garland of flowers in her hands stands beside a pedestal. There is a pitcher at her feet. The face of the woman is painted. Between the outside squares and the picture there is a border of wheat sprays. In one of the lower squares is the inscription: "Ann E Kelly was born in Halifax April 20 in the year of our Lord 1814 and made this sampler in Mrs. Leah Meguier's School in Harrisburg January 21, 1826. O may the Lord instil good principles in me and make me a good and faithful servant." The sampler is wrought in colored silks on cotton. The metallic threads and ribbon border used by Elizabeth Finney in 1807 were not used on this later school sampler, nor is the design as elaborate.

In 1812 Mary Hamilton made a sampler in Mrs. Welchan's School in Maytown, Lancaster County, similar to those embroidered at Leah Galligher's School in Lancaster city and Leah Meguier's School in Harrisburg.[16] The border is made up of a series of squares containing different designs of baskets and sprays of flowers. In an oval frame, in the center, a woman is standing under a tree, her face and arms painted. In a square at the bottom is an inscription again similar to those found at the above-mentioned schools: "Mary Hamilton a daughter of John and Catharine Hamilton was born in County Antrim [Ireland] February the 1 in the year of our Lord 1794 and made this sampler in Maytown in Mrs. Welchan's School in the year of our Lord 1812."

In 1819 a sampler was inscribed: "Mary Fitz daughter of Jacob and Susana Fitz was born in York county September the 24 1807 and made this sampler in Wrightsville in Mrs. Buchanan's School in the year 1819."[17] The border design, similar to those used at Leah Galligher's School in Lancaster, Leah Meguier's School in Harrisburg and Mrs. Welchan's School in Maytown is divided into sixteen compartments containing birds, blowing sprays, baskets of flowers, a house, boys at play and geometric designs. In the center panel there is a design of two ladies in a garden. The hair of the ladies is human hair. Around the border is a green silk ribbon. The sampler was worked in colored silks, on cotton using cross, satin, knots, rococo and stem stitches.

1800 sampler inscribed: "Weston School 9th mo 13th 1800 H P". Embroidered in silk on linen in cross stitch. The colors used are green, tan, black and white. 21″ × 11½″. WESTTOWN SCHOOL.

Westtown Boarding School, in Westtown Township, Chester County, opened on May 6, 1799 with twelve or thirteen students. This school was under the supervision of the Philadelphia Yearly Meeting of the Society of Friends. It was for the children of Friends only, the school's aim being to give the boys and girls a guarded religious education under teachers who were religious men and women dedicated to the principles of the Society of Friends. On 4th Month, 11, 1799 a circular was issued: "INFORMATION For Parents and others inclining to send Children for Education to Friend's boarding school at West-Town" announcing the opening of the school, how to apply, the cost of tuition, listing the clothing necessary for both boys and girls and mentioning: "The girls are also to bring with them a pair of Scissors, Thread-case, Thimble, Work-bag and some plain sewing or knitting to begin with."[18]

> The girls study practically the same subjects as the boys. The chief difference is that sewing is emphasized, and that consequently there is time only for elementary mathematics. Two weeks in six are spent in the sewing school, from which the girls go to reading and writing classes as usual, but during the rest of the time they are busy with the needle. Plain sewing comes first, and darning as well. A piece twelve by eight inches must be so perfectly darned that the mending can scarcely be distinguished from the original material. This examination passed, the students undertake the complex embroidery of spectacle cases, globes representing the earth, and samplers with beautifully stitched designs bordering alphabets and moral sentiments, usually in poetry. Some of the more proficient are allowed to stitch views of the School, to be framed and exhibited as pictures, but this, as well as the making of elaborate samplers, is frowned on by the Committee as "Superfluous," and to be discouraged.[19]
>
> Classes were attended regularly, and time was allowed for learning plain sewing and darning; the more expert graduated to the working of embroidery. Delicate and intricate masterpieces of fancywork served to hold the interest of girls during the time of recreation which, in a later age, would be given over to exercise.[20]

Examples of a variety of different types of needlework worked by the students are known: mending or darning samplers, samplers containing the alphabet, samplers with geometric designs, samplers with pious verses, terrestrial and celestial silk globes and a few pictures of the red brick school building.

The "mending" or "darning" sampler was the first sampler to be made by the students. There were five or seven different darning stitches worked onto the white or sometimes gray-blue linen ground. It was necessary to work pattern darning samplers on a material, such as linen or muslin, that had threads even enough to be counted. The darning stitches would be worked in a contrasting color to the ground. In this way girls were taught a useful skill, that of mending fabrics invisibly. The 1813 darning sampler of Hannah Poole was worked in white on gray-blue linen. [p. 46] The spelling "Weston" for "Westtown" School is quite common. Each of the seven squares has a different darning pattern. The girl's name, name of the school and date were wrought in cross stitch. In 1813 Hannah Poole also embroidered a sampler having the typical Westtown School vine and leaf scroll border and a pious verse worked in black silk on a linen ground. [p. 46]

Extract.

Fountain of Being, teach us to devote
To thee each purpose, action, work and thought,
Thy grace our hope, thy love our only boast,
Be all distinctions in the Christian lost,
Be this in every state our wish alone,
Almighty, wide and good, Thy Will be done.

The lettering is embroidered in cross stitch, the leaves in satin stitch and the vine in a slanting long stitch. A tan colored silk was sometimes used in place of the black silk in the making of these samplers. Samplers worked at the Pleasant Hill Boarding School, at Byberry in Philadelphia, also used the vine and leaf scroll border. Rachel Budd, of Mount Holly, New Jersey, entered Westtown School as pupil # 16 in 1799. Later, in the same year she became a teacher of arithmetic, grammar and writing for £30 a year. In March, 1803 she left the school to marry John Comly, another teacher, who was the author of a well-known "English Grammar" and also a spelling book. This was the first of many Westtown School marriages. As husband and wife they started the Pleasant Hill Boarding School in 1804, and until 1810 it was a boarding school for girls. It is probable that Rachel Comly taught the pupils of Pleasant Hill to make the vine and leaf scroll border that she had learned, as a pupil, at Westtown School.

Other schools are known to have used the scroll and the vine and scroll border. The 1802 sampler of Ruth Jenks, worked at the Plymouth School, Montgomery County, has a similar scroll but not leaves.[21] The 1807 sampler of Phebe Webster wrought at "Downingstown School," Downingtown, Chester County,[22] the 1808

RIGHT. 1813 darning sampler by Hannah Poole worked at the Westtown School in Chester County. Embroidered in white on a gray-blue linen. Her name, school and date are worked in cross stitch. 9½″ × 9½″. THE AUTHOR.

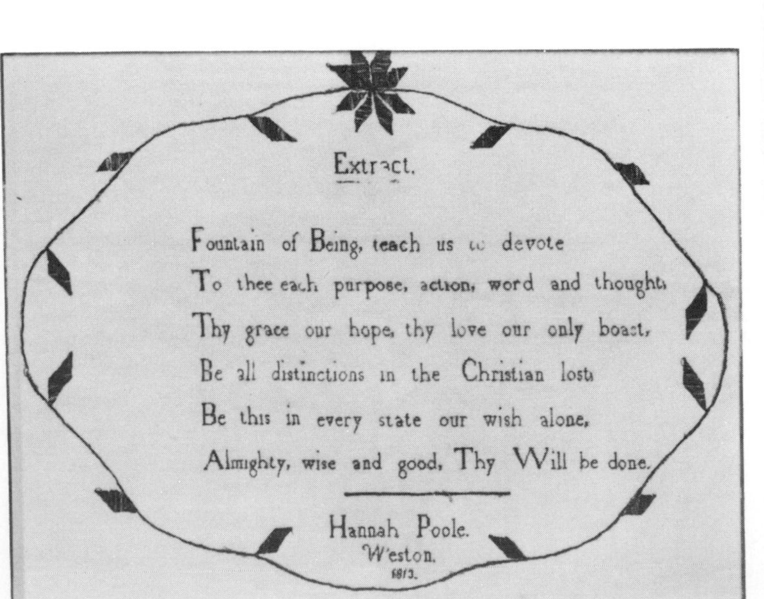

LEFT. 1813 sampler of Hannah Poole worked at the Westtown School in Chester County. Embroidered in black silk on linen using cross, satin and a long slanting stitch. 14″ × 11″. THE AUTHOR.

sampler of Barbary Eagles, worked at the Bristol School, Bucks County,[23] and the 1818 sampler of Rebecca Way worked at the Brandywine Boarding School, Chester County,[24] have vine and leaf scroll borders.

The 1800 cross stitch sampler of Elizabeth Humphreys [p. 50] has four sets of alphabets, two sets of numerals, a small vase of flowers and is inscribed:

> WEST-TOWN SCHOOL
> Blessed is that servant whom his
> lord when he cometh shall find watching

The 1802 sampler of Ann Carlile, Westtown, from Buckingham in Bucks County, is unique in many ways. [p. 48] The vine, without leaves, circling the verses is worked in dark blue silk as is part of the verse itself. The remaining verses are worked in tan silk.

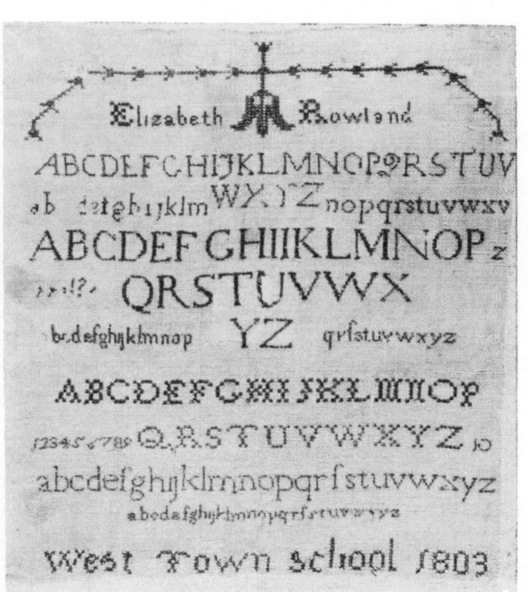

LEFT. 1803 samplers by Elizabeth Rowland worked at the Westtown School in Chester County. Embroidered in black silk on linen in cross stitch. 12″ × 10¼″. WESTTOWN SCHOOL.

RIGHT. Embroidered in silk on linen in cross stitch. The colors used are green, blue, pink, cream, yellow and white. 14½″ × 14½″. CHESTER COUNTY HISTORICAL SOCIETY.

WESTTOWN

O best of parents, wipe your tears
Or rather the Parental Nature pay
The tears of grateful joy who for a while
Lent you this younger self this opening bloom
Of your enlightn'd minds and gentle worth
Believe the muse the wintery blast of death
Kills not the buds of virtue no! they spread
Beneath the heavenly beam of brighter suns
Through endless ages into higher powers

1802 sampler by A Carlile worked at Westtown School in Chester County. Embroidered in silk on linen using cross and satin stitches. The colors used are tan, blue, red, yellow and white. 12″ × 13″. MERCER MUSEUM OF THE BUCKS COUNTY HISTORICAL SOCIETY.

1807 sampler of Elizabeth Finney, worked at Mrs. Leah Meguier's School, in Harrisburg. Embroidered in silk, on muslin, using cross, flat, bullion knot, queen, outline, buttonhole and satin stitches. 22″ × 20″. THE AUTHOR.

Scattered throughout the sampler are names of men and women, some of whom can be identified: Joshua and Ann Sharples became the first permanent superintendent and matron of the school in 1800; Rachel Budd, already mentioned, was a teacher; Martha Baker, an instructor of grammar and sewing; Ann Ingham, a nurse, and Hannah Tunis, Sarah Smith, Elizabeth Folwell, Ruth James, Rachel Scholfield, Rebecca Smith and Edith Sharples were fellow students. Along the border of this sampler are geometric designs.

The geometric cross stitch sampler marked "Weston School 9th mo 13 1800 H P" [p. 43] is unusual as it mentions a day and month as well as a year. The initials are probably those of classmates. Included in the design are bird and floral motifs, sometimes enclosed in garland or tablet patterns neatly spaced on the linen ground.

In 1803 Elizabeth Rowland embroidered two samplers at Westtown School using cross stitch. [p. 47] The first was an alphabet sampler with one set of numerals wrought entirely in black silk on a linen ground. The second sampler mentions "Elizabeth Rowland An Emblem of Innocence 1803 West-Town School" in the center, surrounded by scattered motifs of flowers, birds, animals and baskets of fruit.

Two embroidered pictures of the old school building are most interesting and rare. The first picture [p. 52] has written on the back of the frame: "Supposed to have been the work of Deborah Philips in 1804." This would make it the earliest known embroidered picture of the school. It is worked in silk on a fine linen ground. The border, surrounding the picture, reminds one of the vine and leaf scroll border so frequently employed at Westtown School. In front of the brick school building is a white fence and a row of trees. Another picture was worked by Sarah N. Barton. [p. 52] It is embroidered in silk on a linen ground. There is a complete disregard for proportion and perspective. The bird sitting on the tree is almost as large as the tree, as are some of the animals in the foreground. The whole effect

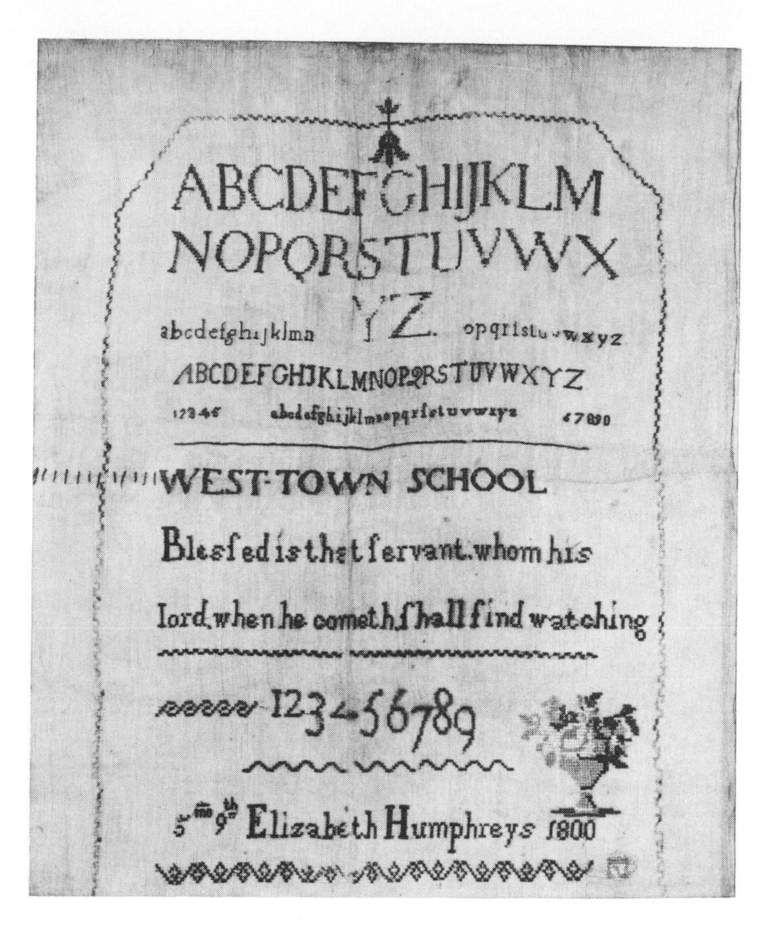

1800 sampler by Elizabeth Humphreys worked at Westtown School in Chester County. Embroidered in silk on linen in cross stitch. The colors used are red, green, tan, black and white. 14½″ × 12½″. WESTTOWN SCHOOL.

is charming. The book *American Samplers* mentions that Martha Heuling of Moorestown, New Jersey, portrayed the school building in 1809.[25] Prancing deer are stitched below the building as well as a verse so faded that it can no longer be read, with a square-shaped vine, at the botton of the sampler. The border has been beautifully worked with baskets of fruit, flowers and abstract motifs.

Celestial and terrestrial silk globes were made by the students. [p. 56] There is very little needlework on the globes. The longitude and latitude lines are couched down and the borders of countries are often worked in the outline stitch. The ships, animals, people and names of the countries, oceans and constellations are painted in black on the silk ground. A girl wrote home in reference to the embroidered globes:

> I expect to have a good deal of trouble in making them, yet I hope that they will recompense me for all my trouble, for they will certainly be a curiosity to you and of considerable use in instructing my brothers and sisters, and to strengthen my own memory, respecting the supposed shape of our earth, and the manner in which it moves (or is moved) on its axis, or the line drawn through it, round which it revolves every 24 hours.[26]

1802 sampler by Sarah Bye worked at Fallsington Boarding School in Bucks County. Embroidered in silk on linen in cross stitch. The colors used are green, brown, tan, red, gray, pink, black and white. 21½″ × 15½″. MRS. J. STOGDELL STOKES.

Sampler by Sarah N. Barton of Westtown School. Embroidered in silk on linen in cross stitch. The colors used are brown, green, tan, black and white. $11\frac{1}{2}'' \times 7''$. WESTTOWN SCHOOL.

Westtown School. Written on the back of the frame: "Supposed to have been the work of Deborah Philips in 1804." Embroidered in silk on fine linen using stem, satin, cross and chain stitches. The colors used are red, green, tan, yellow, black and white. $14\frac{1}{2}'' \times 9\frac{1}{2}''$. WESTTOWN SCHOOL.

The cross stitch sampler worked by Sarah Bye in 1802, at the Fallsington Boarding School, Bucks County, has a balanced spot pattern inside the conventionalized strawberry border. [p. 51] In the center is a garland of flowers surrounded by sprays of flowers, birds, both singly and in pairs, and cornucopias with flowers. Near the bottom of the sampler, to form a division between the spot patterns and the name of the girl, parts of geometric tablets were employed. The Fallsington Boarding School is thought to have been established by Joshua Woolston near the close of the eighteenth century.[27]

In 1802 a sampler was marked: "Dolly Sheller is my name and Dolly Sheller made this lady Lancaster 1802." [p. 54] It is embroidered in silk on a linen ground. In an oval in the center stands a woman holding a ribbon and a garland of flowers over her head. This sampler has a number of unusual features: the woman's hair is human hair; the figure and ribbon are outlined with a twisted metal wire; the earring, necklace and shoe buckles are also made of the twisted wire; sequins decorate the oval and her face and hands are made of paper that was painted and attached to the ground. Around the border is a green ribbon over which a quilled pink ribbon has been sewn. The use of one ribbon sewn over another is rarely encountered.

The Young Ladies' Academy of Philadelphia in 1803 included music and embroidery in its curriculum.

Mr. Kennedy.
To Mrs. Mallon Dr.
Oct. 19, 1803 To 3 Months Tuition & Board of Miss McCoy @

£70 P ann	£17 10
3 months tuition in Music	5 1 3
do Embroidery	2 5
do Washing	2 5[28]

In 1803 Mary McClees worked a sampler at the "Radnor school," in Delaware County. There is a strawberry border around three sides.[29] After 1800 many of the Pennsylvania samplers have borders only on three sides instead of four. She divided her sampler into three sections, using simple cross borders. On the top section she embroidered verses, two birds, two sprays of roses, four groups

1802 sampler marked: "Dolly Sheller is My name and Dolly Sheller made this lady Lancaster 1802". Embroidered in silk on linen using buttonhole, petit point and flat stitches. The colors used are blue, rose, rust and cream. Human hair, sequins and coiled metal wire were used. The face and hands were painted on paper and attached to the linen. Around the border is a green silk ribbon over which a pink quilled ribbon was sewn. $9\frac{1}{2}'' \times 8''$. THE AUTHOR.

of initials and a basket of strawberry plants. In the center section there are verses and two baskets of tulips and in the lower section two baskets of strawberry plants, five groups of initials and a wreath around her name, school and date. This is an interesting school sampler in that it does not include alphabets or numerals.

In 1806 Sarah Brinton made a sampler at the Brandywine school in Chester County in wool on a coarse linen ground.[30] She embroidered a strawberry border, a smaller saw-tooth border and inside the remaining space worked an alphabet, a spray of flowers and this inscription:

> The work in hand my friends may have
> When i am in the silent grave
> Sarah Brintons work Bwine
> school 1806 J AB IB HG LB

She used cross, satin, back and tent stitches.

George Peirce in 1815 founded the Brandywine Boarding School in Chester County.

> The subscriber thinks proper to inform his friends and the public in general, that he has concluded to open a boarding school (for the tuition of Youth) in Brandywine Township, Chester County, and State of Pennsylvania; about five miles northwest from Downington, situate between the Philadelphia and Lancaster and Downingtown, Ephrata and Harrisburg turnpikes, about two miles distant from each, on a high, healthful, and pleasant situation, where are comfortable and convenient accommodation for the purpose.
>
> The youth who may be put under his tuition, will be considered in every respect as a part of his family; and as the number of pupils is not to exceed twenty-five, it will be in his power; and it is his design to pay particular attention to their instruction in the several branches he contemplates teaching; which are Spelling, Reading, Writing (under the

late, and much improved system of writing, by Nathan Towne, of New York,)

Arithmetic	Natural Philosophy
Mensuration	Gauging
Surveying	Trigonometry
Astronomy	Elements of Botany and Chemistry
Bookkeeping	English Grammar
Geometry	History
Geography—use of maps	Composition

A proper attention will also be paid to instruct the girls in Needlework.

Scholars will be admitted for anytime not less than three months; and the terms are $120. per annum, to be paid in quarterly installments, and each payment in advance.

Stationery, &c, will be furnished at the school at the customary prices.

The morals, health and comfort of the scholars will receive a particular and interested attention.

Globes made at the Westtown School, Chester County. Painted and embroidered in silk on silk. WESTTOWN SCHOOL.

N.B. It is desired that the scholars may not be supplied with white, or very light colored apparel, on account of the extra washing. And it is hoped also that parents and others will be particularly careful to send no child under the effect of any infectious disease. Boys will be admitted from eight to fifteen years old, and girls at any age over eight.

School to open the first of the 9th month. Subscriptions will be received by James Way, Philadelphia, and the subscriber

George Peirce-Jun[31]

Emmor Kimber in 1817 established the French Creek Boarding School in Chester County.

The school is situated on the road leading from Norristown to Yellow Springs and is about 27 miles from Philadelphia. A stage is established which affords safe, easy and frequent communication between Philadelphia and the school.

Twenty-four scholars are now in the school, and accommodations are provided for a greater number in the ensuing year.

Sewing	Reading	Writing
Arithmetic	English Grammar	

Geography—use of globes and maps and the French Language are taught.

Terms for tuition and board Fifty dollars a quarter with five dollars a quarter extra for French.

For the accommodation of parents and others having business at the school, there is a house of entertainment on the farm.

Vacation, twice in the year; two weeks in the 4th and two in the 10th month.[32]

School samplers in which the students worked alphabets were very prevalent during the nineteenth century. In 1810 Eliza Kinsey wrought an alphabet sampler at the Buckingham Union School in Bucks County.[33] She used cross and rococo stitches in silk on a linen ground.

Hannah Rennard in 1821 worked a sampler at the Diamond

Rock School in Chester County.[34] She embroidered two alphabets, numerals, name, school name, date and simple cross borders using cross and eyelet stitches. This sampler has no enclosing border, which is unusual.

In 1824 Elizabeth Herrher, at the age of eight years, made a sampler inscribed: "Done in Ruth H. Redman's School, Strawsburg [Strasburg]" in Lancaster County, in cross stitch. She embroidered alphabets, flowerpots, birds and two dogs surrounded by a strawberry border.[35]

The sampler "Markd by Phebe Webster for her sister Eliza Downing 1807 Downingstown School" has the vine and leaf scroll border worked in tan silk on linen.[36] Inside the border the following verses were embroidered:

> When beauty's charms decay,
> as soon they must.
> And all its glories,
> in the dust.
> The virtuous mind beyond
> the reach of time,
> Shall ever blossom in a
> happier clime
> Whose never-fading joys no
> tongue can tell
> Where everlasting youth, and
> beauty dwell.

Samplers mentioning that they were made for a specific person are extremely rare.

In 1812 William Downing advertised:

> WANTED At Downingtown. A SCHOOL MISTRESS, Who understands Grammar, and can instruct Children in Reading, Writing, and Arithmetic, also marking and plain Sewing.[37]

A school for teaching the following branches of needle-work, viz: "Tamborework in shading and in gold and silver; embroidery in all its branches; also, Shenel-work, Felagree-work, open-work, plain sewing, and sampler work; also painting and drawing" was announced in September 1802 by Mrs. Elliott, who lived on East King Street in Lancaster.[38]

Embroidering faces is extremely difficult. The painting and drawing that Mrs. Elliott taught may well have been used by her students in painting faces on the material itself or else in painting faces on a piece of paper and attaching the paper to the sampler. Quite a number of Pennsylvania samplers have been found in which the faces and sometimes the hands and arms are painted. Elizabeth Finney's 1807 sampler [plate II] and Willamina Rine's 1813 sampler [below] have painted faces.

1813 sampler by Willamina Rine worked at Mrs. Armstrong's School in Lancaster. Embroidered in silk on cotton using French knot, cross, stem and satin stitches. The face is painted on the cotton. The colors used are red, blue, yellow, brown, tan and white. 19½″ × 16½″. COURTESY OF THE COOPER UNION MUSEUM.

Caufeild and Saward in *The Dictionary of Needlework* define Tambour Work as being "of Eastern origin, and was worked in China, Persia, India, and Turkey, long before it became known in England . . . In England, Tambour Work (the name of which is derived from the French, and means a drum, in allusion to the shape of the frame used) or Tambouring upon white materials with white thread, became an article of manufacture sixty-years ago, [ca. 1825] and gave employment to the poorer classes in Middlesex, Nottingham, and Ireland . . . For many years English and Continental workers only embroidered in this work upon crêpe, muslin and fine cambric . . ." Tambour work is embroidery in chain stitch executed with a hook instead of a needle on material stretched in a tambour frame.

During the nineteenth century there was a tendency in some schools to expand the curriculum. In 1818, Mrs. Hopkins' School, 163 Spruce Street in Philadelphia advertised:

> With the requisite aid of competent masters, the course of instruction will embrace the English, French, and Italian languages, Writing, Arithmetic, Music, Dancing, Drawing in Crayons . . . Painting on Velvet, Embroidery, Tambour, Plain Sewing and various fashionable fancy works, Sacred History, Ancient and Modern History, Mythology, Chronology, Geography, the Use of Globes and Maps, the Belles-Lettres, Rhetoric, Elocution, Composition, Moral Philosophy, and the Elements of Astronomy and Botany.[39]

In 1808 samplers were embroidered at both the Pleasant Hill Boarding School and the Bristol School using the vine and leaf scroll border that had first been used at the Westtown School. Barbary Eagles, at the Bristol School, Bucks County, embroidered four alphabets inside the scroll and baskets of flowers, sprays of flowers and initials outside the scroll.[40] Julia Knight, at the Pleasant Hill Boarding School at Byberry in Philadelphia, embroidered three alphabets, one wreath enclosing initials, one wreath enclosing a bird and the following verses inside the vine and leaf scroll border.[41]

1824 sampler marked: "Mary Graves was born 2nd mo the 28th 1798 and done this work with Hannah G. Carpenter in the Year of our Lord 1824". Embroidered in silk on linen using cross, satin and petit point stitches. The colors used are green, yellow, blue, brown, black and white. 32″ × 30″. THE AUTHOR.

Remember time will shortly come
When we a strict account must give,
To God the righteous Judge of all
How we upon this earth do live.

Outside the border in each corner of the sampler there is a spray of flowers.

1811 sampler by Hannah Carpenter of Chester County. Embroidered in silk on linen using satin, cross, petit point and rococo stitches. The colors used are green, yellow, blue, brown, tan and black. 29″ × 27″. CHESTER COUNTY HISTORICAL SOCIETY.

During the eighteenth century samplers had included names of members of the family (Mary Morris, 1727) and had mentioned the names of fathers and mothers (Lydia Hoopes, 1765 and Hannah Fletcher, 1793). In the nineteenth century the true genealogical type sampler was embroidered listing father, mother, brothers and sisters and often the date they were born and if dead, the date of death. These samplers were a record and frequently took the place of the Family Bible for that purpose.

The 1811 sampler of Hannah Carpenter, worked at the age of twenty-two, is extremely large. [p. 62] Many samplers, worked at this period, are larger than those embroidered during the eighteenth century. In the center Hannah Carpenter worked her name, the date she was born and the year she made the sampler, all enclosed in a garland. Inside squares and rectangles she embroidered the names and dates of birth of her parents, brothers and sisters in addition to pious verses. The design of the sampler is balanced. The spot motifs include pyramid and weeping willow trees, baskets and vases of flowers, birds perched on either side of a basket, various initials and a Tree of Life. The whole is enclosed with a simple scroll pattern with a few leaves and strawberries. The frame of the sampler is unique. In the top section there is a silhouette of Hannah Carpenter, and two water color pictures, one of her home and one of the nearby barn.

It had become the custom for girls to sign their work as a testament to their proficiency. In some instances the names of the instructress was also included. In a garland there is inscribed "Mary Graves was born 2nd mo the 28th 1798 and done this work with Hannah G. Carpenter in the Year of our Lord 1824". [p. 61] Mary Graves' sampler is quite similar to the 1811 sampler of Hannah Carpenter. Enclosed in squares and rectangles are her parents' and brothers' names with dates of birth and pious verses. The design is balanced, having in the center a shepherdess, sheep, hills and trees. Surrounding the rural scene are vases of flowers, Trees of Life, weeping willow trees and birds on either side of a basket of flowers. The border of vines, leaves and flowers is much more elaborate than the simple border used by Hannah Carpenter thirteen years earlier. Comparatively few teachers' names have been recorded on the Pennsylvania samplers.

In England, pictures of maps, worked on a linen, silk or satin ground, were common. They were mainly worked during the eighteenth century and seem to have been a part of school exercises. Frequently the maps were surrounded by an embroidered floral border. The names of towns, the compass and sometimes ships were drawn in ink on the background material.

American map samplers are extremely rare. As in England, Pennsylvania embroidered maps were worked at schools, enabling the students to combine the study of geography with that of needlework. The "Map of the united States" embroidered by Mary H. Walter, at Mrs. Given's School in Brandywine Township, Chester County [p. 65], shows the eastern states bordered by Upper and Lower Canada, the Atlantic Ocean, the Mississippi River and Louisiana. The lines for the borders of the states, the compass and the place names are wrought in very fine petit point stitch in black silk. The flowers around the border, in the English tradition, are embroidered in shades of green, blue, yellow, pink, brown, gold, black and white, using satin, long and short, stem and chain stitches. The whole picture has a cream colored quilled silk ribbon border.

At Westtown School, in Chester County, the students in the early nineteenth century made terrestrial and celestial silk globes. [p. 56] There is little needlework on the globes. The longitude and latitude lines are couched down and the borders of countries are worked in the outline stitch. The ships, animals, people and names of countries and oceans are painted in black on the ground. Sometimes the globes were set into small stands made especially for them.

An interesting map of Pennsylvania was made about 1840.

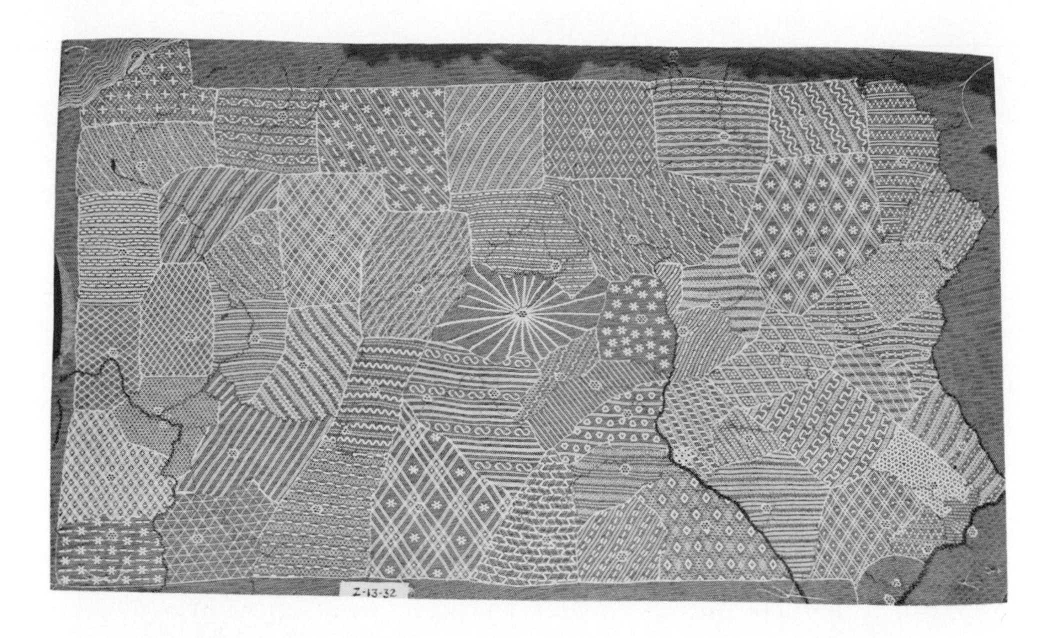

Map of Pennsylvania. Circa 1840. Needle-made lace patterns on a net ground. 26″ × 15″. HISTORICAL SOCIETY OF PENNSYLVANIA.

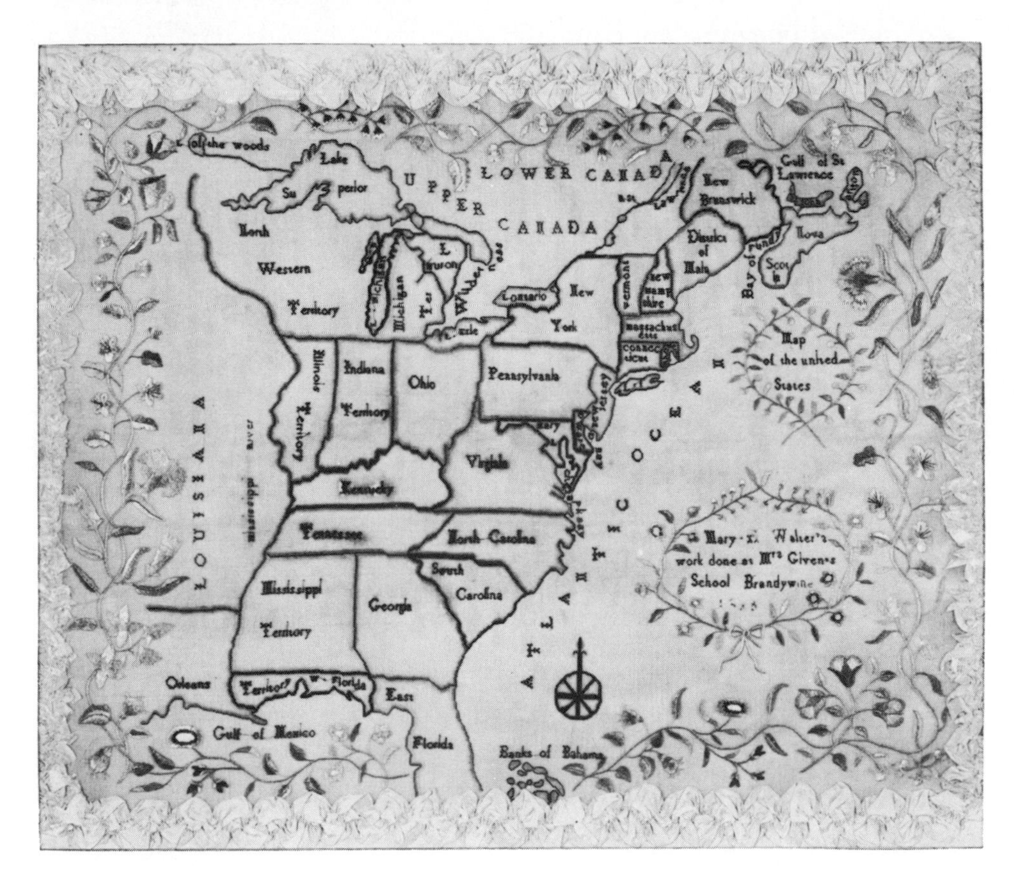

1813 "Map of the united States" by Mary H. Walter worked at Mrs. Given's School, Brandywine, Chester County. Embroidered in silk on linen using petit point, satin, long and short, stem and chain stitches. The colors used are green, blue, yellow, pink, brown, gold, black and white. Around the border is a quilled cream-color ribbon. 24″ × 20″. CHESTER COUNTY HISTORICAL SOCIETY.

[p. 65] The different counties of the state have been identified by the use of various stitches wrought on the net ground. This is the only known example of a map depicting Pennsylvania exclusively as well as the only map found to have been worked on a net ground. It was probably embroidered at a girls' school.

Two sisters attended Mrs. Armstrong's School in Lancaster where they embroidered samplers. In 1808 Fanny Rine, age twelve years, worked a vine and flower border on three sides of her sampler, using satin and cross stitches.[42] In the center a wreath encloses a girl with a lamb sitting under a willow tree. There are sprays of flowers in the four corners and underneath the scene an inscription, alphabets and verses.

Fanny Rine, a daughter of Christian and Barbara Rine, was born in the borough of Lancaster the 26th day of Sept. 1796 and made this sampler in Mrs. Armstrong's School A.D. 1808.

> Teach me the measure of my days
> Thou maker of my fame
> I would survey life narrow space
> And learn how frail I am

In the following verses she quoted the Reverend Isaac Watts, Psalm XIII

> The Lord my shepherd is
> I shall be well supply'd
> Since he is mine and I am his
> What can I want beside
>
> He leads me to the place
> Where heav'ny pasture grows
> Where living waters gently pass
> And full salvation flows

The stars which in their courses roll
Have much instruction given
But thy good work informs by soul
How I may get to heav'n

In 1813 Willamina Rine, age six years, embroidered her sampler. [p. 59] Surrounded by sprays of leaves and flowers tied with bows, a girl holding a bouquet of flowers stands under a weeping willow tree. The face of the girl is painted on the cotton ground. Underneath she worked "Willamina Rine a daughter of Christian and Barbara Rine was born November 6th 1801 and Made this Sampler at Mrs. Armstrong's School, Lancaster" and the first verses found on Fanny Rine's sampler. The sampler was embroidered in silk, using cross, stem, satin and French knot stitches. Fanny and Willamina Rine were probably girls of German or Swiss descent, known in Pennsylvania as Pennsylvania Dutch.

Elizabeth Witty, of Pittsburgh, in 1842 embroidered a sampler that is in many ways reminiscent of the sampler wrought by Willamina Rine just mentioned. [p. 68] In the center a girl holds a basket of flowers and stands under a willow tree. Above, a butterfly and bird fly. The border has vine, leaves, buds and flowers. During the nineteenth century the willow tree was used more than any other tree in needlework.

Two samplers are known that were made at the North School in Philadelphia. In 1812 Hannah D. Lambert worked seven alphabets in black, using the stem and cross stitches.[43] Around the border was a vine with leaves and at the top hangs an inverted tulip. In 1821 Cornelia A. Smith, of Philadelphia, embroidered four alphabets, two baskets with fruit, two stars and the same border with inverted tulip, using cross and eyelet stitches in blue, black, pink, green, brown and yellow silk.[44] Both samplers are similar to that worked in 1800 by Elizabeth Humphreys, at Westtown School in Chester County. [p. 50]

In 1818 Mary Coles at the Ellisburg School near Philadelphia worked a sampler using stem, satin and cross stitches.[45] There is a floral border on three sides with name, date and small birds in the

1842 sampler by Elizabeth Witty of Pittsburgh. Embroidered in wool on linen using back, feather, petit point, cross, outline and satin stitches. The colors used are brown, mustard, olive, pink, blue, beige, green and yellow. $16\frac{3}{4}'' \times 13\frac{1}{4}''$. COURTESY OF THE MUSEUM OF ART, CARNEGIE INSTITUTE. GIFT OF MYRTLE HOEY BURNS.

top center. At the bottom there is a house with conventionalized trees and small animals. Detached designs of flowers, baskets and birds and verses fill in the remaining space.

No longer I follow a sound
No longer a dream I pursue
O happiness now to be found
Unattainable treasure Adieu

In the first quarter of the nineteenth century in Pennsylvania a number of samplers were wrought, the patterns of which consist of scattered formal or naturalistic flowers and leaves, geometric motifs, birds and initials enclosed in garlands or tablet patterns. To form borders sections of the garland or tablet patterns were employed.

The earliest sampler of this type was worked in cross stitch by an unknown girl at "Weston School" in 1800. [p. 43] Single birds, birds in pairs and initials are enclosed in garlands and tablet patterns. In 1802 Sarah Bye at Fallsington School used parts of tablets to form a division in her spot pattern sampler. [p. 51] The 1818 sampler of Rebecca Ingram of Downingtown was worked in cross, eyelet and rococo stitches.[46] In the garlands and tablets she embroidered a bird eating a strawberry, a swan and her name. Scattered throughout are initials and both stylized and naturalistic floral motifs. The 1819 sampler of "Hannah Wilson West Marlborough School" in Chester County has her name enclosed in the vine and leaf scroll motif,[47] found on many Westtown School samplers. To it she added a bow at the bottom. In this sampler parts of garlands and tablets have been used only to form the border. The center has tulips and roses growing in tubs, a willow tree, two birds sitting on another tree, strawberries, the name of her mother and father, and possibly the name of her instructor, Edith Baily. The sampler is wrought using cross, satin and stem stitches.

In 1818 Margaret Bowman worked a sampler in cross stitch at the "Merion B [oarding] School."[48] On three sides there is a strawberry and vine border and in the center the following verses:

Extract
JESUS permit thy gracious name to stand,
As the first effort of a females hand,
And while her fingers o'er the canvass move,
Engage her tender heart thy love

Scattered throughout the remaining area are sprays of flowers, fruit in baskets, swans and a bouquet of flowers tied with a bow. Lower Merion Academy, built in 1812, was founded through the will of Jacob Jones who left a certain messuage or parcel of land and eight hundred pounds for the erection of a building to be used as a schoolhouse and a dwelling for a tutor or tutors and another five hundred pounds to be placed by them on land security for the support of a school at which a certain number of poor and orphan children should be educated free of charge. It was a boarding school and also had day pupils. From the beginning there was no distinction as to sex.[49]

During the nineteenth century the girls showed a marked tendency to depict, in architecture, the imposing and elegant. The 1819 sampler of Jane Hyland of Columbia, Lancaster County, has a house of the latest style, the two chimneys joined by a balustrade, two palladian windows and a double door over which there is a fan light. On the left of the house there is a terrace with a pot of flowers. [p. 71] A woman carrying a bouquet, a swan, a garden bench, a dog, trees and grape vines are on the lawn. The woman's hair is real hair and her collar is made of tinsel thread. There are baskets of flowers on either side of the inscription which states that Sarah McCardell was Jane Hyland's tutoress. The simple border is formed of triangles worked in satin stitch. Swans and garden furniture are seldom depicted in needlework.

In 1822 Hannah E. Moore at the "Easton School" embroidered an architectural sampler using stem, tent, satin and cross stitches.[50] She wrought a floral border on three sides. Inside the border is a house, trees, path, fence, birds and sheep on a terraced lawn. A wreath of flowers encloses verses and there are flowers in pots and detached sprays of flowers in the remaining space.

The 1825 sampler of Sarah Elizabeth Cooper, of Chester County, is wrought in silk and wool on linen. [p. 72] It has a picture

1819 sampler by Jane Hyland of Columbia in Lancaster County. Sarah McCardell, tutoress. Embroidered in silk on linen using cross, satin, stem, French knot and buttonhole stitches. The hair is real and the collar is made of metallic thread. The colors used are pink, green, yellow, brown, orange and white. 20½″ × 16½″. CHESTER COUNTY HISTORICAL SOCIETY.

of a house with a gable roof, sash windows with shutters, a front door over which there is a fan light and there is an elliptical window in the attic. On the lawn stands a woman over half as large as the house, a chair and a basket. She has long flowing wool threads for hair. Enclosing the lawn there is an iron fence with an elaborate gate. On either side of the picture there are baskets in which flowering plants grow. Green ribbon over which diagonal lines of sequins have been sewn forms the rather unique border. The woman's earring is a sequin as is the door knocker on the house.

1825 sampler by Sarah Elizabeth Cooper of Chester County. Embroidered in silk and wool on linen using cross, satin and stem stitches. The colors used are green, blue, yellow, beige and white. Around the edge is a green ribbon border with sequin decoration. 23″ × 21″. CHESTER COUNTY HISTORICAL SOCIETY.

Mary Ann Leiper of Philadelphia marked a sampler "August 11th 1824 Washington and Lafayette Welcome."[51] She worked four alphabets, a floral and vine border at the top and bottom and the following verses:

> When I can read my title clear
> To mansions in the sky
> I bid farewell to every fear
> And wipe my weeping eyes.
>
> Still the orphan & the stranger
> Still the widow owns thy care
> Screened by the[e] in every danger
> Heard by the[e] in every prayer.

The first verses are by the Reverend Isaac Watts.

Eagles are a motif rarely found on Pennsylvania samplers. In 1825 Margaret Moss of Philadelphia, at the age of eleven years, wrought a sampler having an elaborate conventionalized flower border.[52] In the center is a scene which includes a brick house, weeping willow trees on either side and pine trees behind the house; a beehive, a boy tending sheep, two girls, ducks, a dog, cows and a man and woman. Above this country scene there is an American eagle with a wreath on either side, enclosing the name and age of the maker in one and the inscription "Elizabeth Wiert, aged 80, died 1825" in the other. Above the eagle are the words "E Pluribus Unum" and detached figures of angels and stars. The depicting of angels on samplers is extremely rare.

In 1830 Juli Ann Crespin embroidered a sampler at the West Chester School in Chester County. There was a strawberry border on three sides. A verse is enclosed in a heart-shaped border of pink rosebuds and leaves. At the bottom of the sampler she worked a brick house, trees and a lawn.[53]

Two extremely interesting samplers were worked in Lancaster County, in 1822, by two sisters. [p. 75] They are embroidered in silk on a fine linen ground using satin, outline and cross stitches. Ann Barr wrought an alphabet, numerals from one to three, a man playing a musical instrument while two couples dance, verses, and at the bottom two parrots sit on flower plants on either side of a man and woman. The man is elaborately dressed with three large feathers in his hat and he is smoking a pipe that reaches down to his knees.

Her sister, Fanny Barr, embroidered two men on horseback, one of which she labeled "The Looby who presumes to ride". Between the two horsemen there are floral motifs, butterflies and a bird. Near the center of the sampler there are verses and at the bottom two birds on flower plants on either side of a man playing a musical instrument while one couple dances. There is one alphabet but no numerals. Both samplers have a border on three sides only. The samplers of Ann and Fanny Barr are the only Pennsylvania samplers that have been found thus far to include men playing musical instruments while couples dance and to have horsemen depicted.

During the nineteenth century a number of different churches were embroidered in needlework. In 1823 Nancy Johnston, of York, at twelve years of age finished her sampler of Christ Lutheran Church, in York, using cross, flat and eyelet stitches on a linen ground in shades of blue, green, black, yellow, gray, brown, pink and white. [p. 76] Years later she married the Reverend John Canes, minister of the Church. The border is formed of zigzag lines and conventionalized flowers. In the upper corners a bird perches on a simply worked border containing two alphabets, the girl's name, date, and name of her residence. In the lower section the church is embroidered and what is probably the parsonage, a gate, a picket fence and two trees separating the two buildings.

The 1838 sampler of Sarah Ann Dreisback, of Bethlehem,

1822 samplers by Fanny and Ann Barr of Lancaster County. Both are embroidered in silk on linen using satin, stem and cross stitches. The colors used are brown, tan, pink, green and yellow. 23″ × 18½″. LANCASTER COUNTY HISTORICAL SOCIETY.

includes a church, two houses, two trees, a flock of sheep and a bird. [p. 77] The picture has charm, showing a complete lack of perspective: the bird is as large as one house. In the lower section there are verses:

> Amidst the Cheerful bloom of youth
> With ardent zeal pursue
> The ways of Piety and truth
> With death and heaven in view

1823 sampler by Nancy Johnston. The Church is Christ Lutheran in York. Embroidered in silk on linen using cross and eyelet stitches. The colors used are blue, green, yellow, gray, brown, pink, black and white. 18″ × 17″. HISTORICAL SOCIETY OF YORK COUNTY.

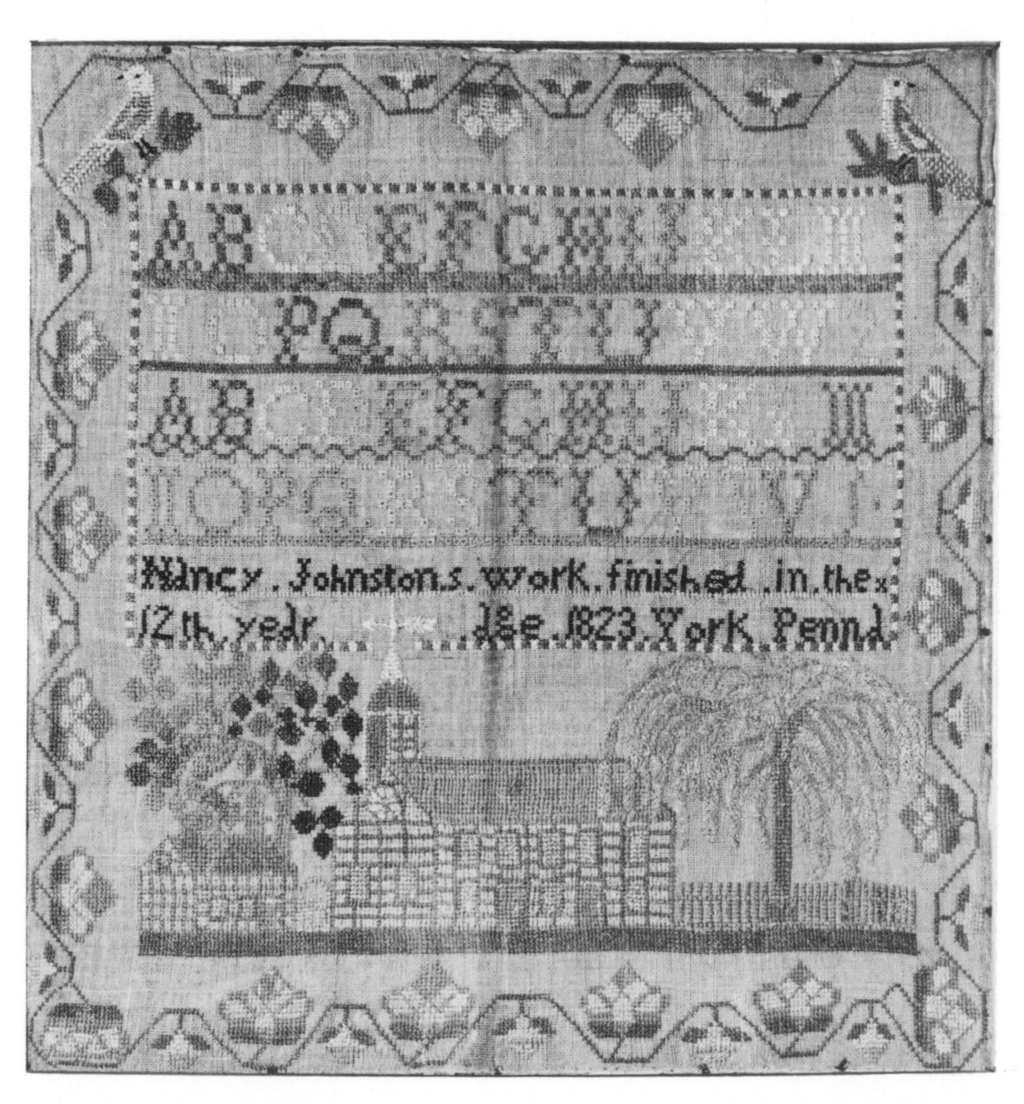

1838 sampler by Sarah Ann Dreisbach of Bethlehem. Embroidered in wool on linen using cross and satin stitches. The colors used are red, pink, yellow, green, blue, brown, gold, tan, gray, burnt orange and white. 17½″ × 25″. MORAVIAN MUSEUM OF BETHLEHEM.

An urn is on either side of the verses; one with flowers and one with strawberries. Around the whole is a very colorful wide floral border. The sampler is almost entirely worked in petit point. Satin stitches were used only on the willow tree and the urns.

In 1824 Lydia Marshall, of Chester County, embroidered a sampler that mentioned her parents' names, her brothers' and sisters' names with their birth dates, her own name, date she was born and the year she worked the sampler: "And done this work in the year 1824" and the name Mary Ann Cheyney, who was probably her teacher. [p. 79] The sampler is well balanced in design and is quite typical of the genealogical samplers of this period.

In 1790 Susanna Muhlenburg of Trappe had worked a Family Record which also included three alphabets, a strawberry border on three sides, a fret border and the following record and verses:[54]

Henry M. Muhlenburg born 1711, died 1787
Ann Mary Weifer born 1727
Philip Hall B. 1733 and Catharine Seckel Born 1728
Henry Muhlenburg Born 1753
Catharine Hall Born 1756
Catharine Muhlenburg Born 1776
Susanna B. 1779
Phillip B 1784
Peter Born 1786
Maria Born 1789
Elizabeth Born 1791
F. Augustus B. 1795

Behold this early sampler may
Show Readers at a future day
That I was taught before too late
All Sorts of idleness to hate

Family Records or Registers such as this did not become usual until the nineteenth century.

While attending the Northern Liberty School, in Philadelphia, in 1827 Jan Sharp made a cross stitch sampler having a tulip border with a rosebud and a bird in the center.[55] Scattered about are vases and sprays of flowers and two butterflies.

The 1830 sampler of Harriet Weiser, a girl of German descent, is most unusual. [p. 80] There is a strawberry border and inside that a smaller saw-tooth border. At the bottom she embroidered a house with a weeping willow tree on either side and on the lawn strawberry plants, two birds holding a heart, dogs and other animals. Above the house are the initials "D W. S W", probably for the names of her parents. The house may well have been her own. In the center is a vase of flowers, a castle, a summer house or pavilion, strawberry plants, hearts and baskets of fruit. In the top half of the sampler Harriet Weiser wrought many scattered motifs including a girl with an anchor, cornucopias, pairs of doves, basket of fruit, hearts, floral sprays, a wreath around her name and date, initials and geometric patterns.

In the early part of the nineteenth century there were many established schools and others opening which included in the curriculum the study of needlework, both plain and ornamental. In 1827 in Chester County, which was a typical area, three schools advertised that they were opening.

1824 sampler by Lydia Marshall of Chester County. Embroidered in silk on linen using cross and petit point stitches. The colors used are cream, gold, blue, green, brown and black. 22″ × 16″. CHESTER COUNTY HISTORICAL SOCIETY.

1830 sampler by Harriet Weiser. Embroidered in silk on linen using cross, petit point, satin and rococo stitches. The colors used are blue, green, brown, tan and white. $18\frac{1}{2}'' \times 27''$.
TITUS C. GEESEY.

Arrangements have been made for opening, on or about the 1st of April next in the borough of West Chester, a school for the instruction of GIRLS, in Reading, Writing, and the rudiments of Arithmetic and Geography; but more particularly in NEEDLEWORK, plain and ornamental. The Proposed Teacher, Mrs. Sarah Taylor, has had several years experience in her profession, and no doubt is entertained that entire satisfaction will be given to her employers. She will board the pupils if preferred, and her undivided attention will be given to the School.[56]

The Downingtown Boarding School For Girls opened August 27, 1827. The curriculum like most other schools of the day included:

English
Natural Philosophy
English and French Languages
Boarding and tuition $30
Washing 36 cents a dozen
The Mathematical Sciences
Botany
Needlework
Drawing

Reading books are kept for the use of the students; other books, stationary etc., at the usual prices.

The school is well supplied with philosophical apparatus.[57]

The West Chester Boarding School For Girls was established by Philip and Rachel Price in 1830 when they advertised the following:

The buildings have been planned expressly with a view to promote comfort of the pupils; —There is a daily communication by stage with the city of Philadelphia and Lancaster, and three times a week with Baltimore.—The course of instruction embraces

Orthography
Arithmetic
Plain Needle work
Chemistry
Bookkeeping
Reading
Geography
History
Natural Philosophy
Composition
Writing
Grammar
Astronomy
Algebra
Geometry

Terms for tuition in the above branches, Boarding, Lodging, and Washing, the use of Reading class books, Maps, Globes, and Library will be $50 per quarter of 12 weeks.

French extra per q.	$5
Drawing and Painting	$5

Each pupil must furnish her own towels.[58]

The Mantua Female Academy in Chester County advertised in 1830 that

> This Institution is now open for the reception of Young Ladies to be instructed in the following branches, viz.—

Reading	Music	Arithmetic
History	Writing	Chronology
English Grammar	Astronomy	Composition
Natural and Moral Philosophy	Rhetoric	Bookkeeping
	Drawing	Painting

Plain and ornamental Needle Work

> The situation is a beautiful and healthy part of Chester County —immediately on the Philadelphia and Lancaster turnpike—42 miles from the former city. The school is under the care and superintendence of the Reverend James Latta; and instruction in it will be given by Miss M'Cullough.
>
> Bible instruction will be given once a week and strict attention will be paid to the morals, manners, and health of the students.
>
> Each quarter will consist of 12 weeks and the charges for that time of tuition, Boarding, Washing, will be $22.50 for which $20 in advance will be taken; and small extra charge to the use of a piano.[59]

The Uwchlan Boarding School For Girls advertised in 1832.

> IS situate in Chester county, Pennsylvania, 25 miles from Philadelphia . . .
>
> The following branches are taught:
>
> Spelling, Reading, Writing, English Grammar, History, Geography, with the use of Globes—Arithmetic, Algebra, some branches of

> Natural Philosophy, viz: Astronomy, Botany, Mineralogy, &c, reading and translating the French Language, plain sewing and knitting, with various kinds of needle & bead work: the price of boarding, washing, &c. with the above branches will be 25 dollars per quarter . . .[60]

In 1834 Miss Palmyra C. Evans announced that she

> Has rented the commodious and airy apartments in the second story of Friends Brick Meeting House, in West Chester, for the purpose of commencing and establishing an English School, in which will be taught Spelling, Reading, Writing, Arithmetic, English Grammar and Geography.
>
> Little girls whose parents may wish it will also be instructed in Plain Sewing and Marking; and their attention directed to correct deportment.
>
> For the three first branches named the terms will be $2.50 per quarter.[61]

The same year:

> Mrs. Smith begs leave to inform the inhabitants of West Chester and its vicinity, that she intends reopening her school on Monday the 30th of June. Mrs. Smith returns sincere thanks for past patronage and respectfully solicits a continuance of the same.

Terms per quarter: Instruction in Reading, Writing, Arithmetic, History, Geography, Grammar, Composition, and Needle-work	$ 4.00
Bead and fancy rug work	1.00
Ornamental Crêpe work	2.00
Music	10.00
Drawing and Painting	8.00
Drawing	5.00
Singing	5.00
French	5.00[62]

In 1839 Mrs. Heath advertised that she gave lessons in needlework, drawing and painting.

> A CARD, MRS HEATH, respectfully informs the inhabitants of West Chester, that she proposes to form classes of young ladies for instruction in the following branches; DRAWING and PAINTING, PAINTING ON VELVET, LACE and SATIN EMBROIDERY, and EMBOSSED and fancy NEEDLE-WORK . . .[63]

The word embossed means embroidery in which the design is in relief. This is done by either stuffing with layers of thread or succession of stitches underneath the embroidery, or else by working over a pad made with thick materials.

By 1849 Miss Palmyra C. Evans had become principal of a newly formed school.

> WEST CHESTER FEMALE SEMINARY
> Miss P. C. Evans, Principal
> THIS institution is located in the unusually pleasant healthy borough of West Chester, Chester county, Pa., to which access is had daily from the east and west by railroad.
>
> Tuition embraces all the branches of a thorough English education, viz: Orthography, Reading, Writing, Grammar, Geography, Practical and Rational Arithmetic, Book-keeping, Algebra and Geometry; Natural, Ancient and Modern History; Intellectual, Moral and Natural Philosophy; Astronomy, Chemistry, Composition, Botany, Physiology, Plain and ornamental Needle Work; in additional instruction will be given in Drawing, Painting, and in the Latin, French and German Languages.
>
> TERMS—Tuition and Boarding, including Washing, $75 per session of 5 months, Drawing, Music and the Languages at moderate extra charge.
>
> The Summer Session will commence on the 1st of May. Circulars will be forwarded on application to the Principal, or H. S. Evans.[64]

The earliest of school lessons consists in learning the alphabet. Rebecca G. McCord in 1833, at the age of eleven, worked five alphabets of capital and small letters and two sets of numerals from one to nine on her sampler. [p. 120] She also included the "Litiz seminary" building itself with a vase of flowers on either side. In the front yard are two dogs which belonged to the headmistress. The sampler is embroidered in silk on a very coarse linen.

In 1822 Elizabeth Miskey, aged eleven years, wrought a sampler in colored silk and wool on coarse brown linen, using chain, stem, rococo and cross stitches.[65] The inscription reads: "Respectfully presented to Anthony and Elizabeth Miskey done in her twelfth year Philadelphia, April 26th 1822." Inside a flower border she embroidered verses, flowering sprays, violet plants and a basket of fruit and flowers.

The cross stitch sampler wrought by Elizabeth Smith, at the Germantown Boarding School in 1835, is an excellent example of

1835 sampler by Elizabeth Smith worked at the Germantown Boarding School in Germantown. Embroidered in silk on linen in cross stitch. The colors used are yellow, green, blue and black. 18″ × 16½″. MRS. ROBERT WILLIAMS TRUMP.

the flowery expressions of gratitude, in verse, worked by many girls at this period. [p. 85]

> To My Parents
> For you who watch'd my dawning soul,
> With rapturous delight,
> And by affection's soft control
> Oft won me to the right.
>
> I'll twine my wreath of flowers and say
> How pure, how deep, how true,
> The current of affection rolls
> From my young heart to you.
>
> This lively garland let it speak
> My gratitude and love,
> Its hues tho' bright yet soon to fade
> An emblem, cannot prove.

1842 sampler by Mary Ann Baily of Chester County. Embroidered in wool on linen using cross, satin and stem stitches. The colors used are red, purple, blue, green, brown, black and white. There is a green ribbon border on four sides and a rosette in each corner. 21″ × 25½″. THE AUTHOR.

Elizabeth Smith was the daughter of Hannah Fletcher, who wrought a sampler in 1793 which has been mentioned. [p. 32]

In many later genealogical samplers willow trees shade monuments which closely resemble the tombs so often found on the embroidered silk mourning pictures of the period. Mary Caley's 1837 sampler mentions her parents, brothers and sisters. [below] Ann, whose name is embroidered in a black square, is thought to have died. Inside a second garland are the following verses:

> Selected.
> While on this glowing canvass stands
> The labour of my youthful hands
> It may remain when I am gone
> For you my friends to look upon.

1837 sampler by Mary Caley of Chester County. Embroidered in silk and chenille on linen using cross, bullion knot, satin and stem stitches. The colors used are green, pink, blue, brown, yellow, black and white. Around three sides there is quilled green ribbon and two rosettes. 32″ × 27″. CHESTER COUNTY HISTORICAL SOCIETY.

The lower section of the sampler has terra firma on which there are a tomb shaded by a weeping willow tree, three sheep, one deer, a squirrel and a rabbit. Two large baskets of flowers are placed on top of the ground. Scattered throughout are floral motifs and two butterflies. There are both flower and quilled ribbon borders on three sides. The sampler was worked using silk, chenille and crinkled silk on a linen ground. This sampler is large, thirty-two by twenty-seven inches, which is typical of samplers worked during this period. Eighteenth century samplers were often less than half the size of Mary Caley's sampler.

Mary Ann Baily's 1842 sampler includes the picture of a mansion house, a tenant house, a flock of sheep, a cow, a dog and a variety of different trees worked in Berlin wool. [p. 86] Both post and rail fences enclose the lawn. There is a basket of strawberries and one of flowers on either side of the verses which are typical of the period and similar to those worked by Mary Caley.

> This work perhaps my friends may have
> When I am in my silent grave
> And which when e'er they chance to see
> May kind remembrance picture me
> While on the glowing canvass stands
> The labour of my youthful hands

The sampler mentions her mother, father and grandparents. The mentioning of the latter is rather infrequently found on samplers. On three sides of the picture there is a floral border and around the four sides a green ribbon with a rosette in each corner. This is the latest sampler found thus far having the quilled ribbon border or rosettes.

The samplers of Sarah Ann Dreisback and Mary Ann Baily are very typical of those worked during the Victorian period. Both are embroidered, using bright analine-dyed Berlin wool.

CREWEL

IN speaking of crewel work Caufeild and Saward in *The Dictionary of Needlework* state: "In early times [it was] known as Caddis, Cadis, or Crule. Derived from the Anglo-Saxon Cleow, afterwards changed to Clew (a ball of thread), and subsequently called Cruell, or Krewel, old German Kleuel. Worsted yarn loosely twisted, employed in the sixteenth century for embroidery on linen textiles, curtains, and household furniture, and also for decorating the dresses of the lower orders; but now extensively for embroidery. It is to be had in every colour, and is made in three sizes and known as tapestry crewel, very soft and even . . . The proper definition of Crewel Work is embroidery upon linen, twilled cotton or stuffs, the foundation material being in most cases left as an unworked background . . ." The *Oxford English Dictionary* defines "crewel" as "thin worsted yarn of two threads used for tapestry and embroidery." During the twentieth century the word crewel has been used to designate either a certain stitch or embroidery in two-ply wool on almost any fabric.

Crewel embroidery became extremely popular in England during the seventeenth century. The East India Company imported the painted or printed cottons known as palimpores from India. The English women wrought variations of the polychrome designs found on the calico hangings in needlework. Especially popular were the Tree of Life designs, detached floral motifs, coiling branches and stems, exotic flowers, large leaves, mounds or hillocks and Chinese motifs.

The designs were frequently quite solidly worked on a twill weave of cotton or a combination of cotton and linen.

In America, crewel-work was a specialty of the women in New England. Few examples of Pennsylvania crewel embroidery are known. Sets of bed and window curtains, bed coverlets and women's dresses, although often made in New England, have not been found in Pennsylvania. The articles which are known to have been embroidered in Pennsylvania include a valance, needlecases, pockets, pot holders, pictures, a child's dress and a wall pocket. They are embroidered in lovely gay colors on either a linen or homespun ground using few stitches. The designs are open and usually include floral motifs. One of the main sources of inspiration for embroidery comes from the land, its trees, fruits, flowers, insects, birds and animals. Flowers were the most popular motif and those most frequently encountered in Pennsylvania needlework are the rose, carnation and tulip.

All the dyes used in the early days except for indigo were garnered from the woods and fields: red from madder; yellow and brown from the bark of butternut, red oak and hickory; crimson from the juice of pokeberry boiled with alum; green from a decoction of goldenrod flowers mixed with indigo and alum; yellow and orange from sassafras bark. The deep blue indigo was bought from a pedlar or from a store. The blue and white crewel work, found in New England, has not been found in Pennsylvania.

A valance marked "I H 1744" is the earliest dated piece of crewel work that has been found.[1] It was embroidered by a member of the Hibberd family of Chester. Flowers, buds and flowers growing from a curving vine were simply and sparsely worked in outline, bullion knots, romanian and cross stitches in shades of red, gold and blue. A number of small birds, one with cherries in its beak, are included in the design.

The outside of the needlecase marked "M D 1766" is embroidered in Florentine stitch and the inside is worked in wool on a linen ground. [below] The initials and date, as in all other Pennsylvania examples found thus far, are worked in cross stitch. As is typical of Pennsylvania crewel few stitches are employed on a given embroidery. On the needlecase French knots, stem, satin and cross stitches were used.

The pairs of pot holders initialed and dated "H M 1775" and "H G 1776" are wrought in wool on a homespun ground. [p. 92] As in the needlecase the embroideress worked roses, carnations and leaves. Other pot holders, very similar to the ones photographed, have been found in Chester County.

LEFT. Needlecase worked in Florentine stitch, in wool, on canvas. The colors used are yellow, red, pink, green, blue and purple. 13″ × 3″. CHESTER COUNTY HISTORICAL SOCIETY.

RIGHT. Needlecase marked "M D 1766". Outside worked in Florentine stitch, in wool, on canvas. The inside worked in wool, on linen, using stem, French knot, satin and cross stitches. The colors used are yellow, blue, green, pink, rust and lavender. 11″ × 4″. WESTTOWN SCHOOL.

Crewel work pot holders initialed and dated "H M 1775" and "H G 1776". Embroidered in wool, on linen, using satin, stem, feather, bullion knot and chain stitches. The colors used are red, pink, green and black. H. $6\frac{1}{2}$", W. $4\frac{1}{2}$" to $5\frac{1}{2}$". MRS. JOSEPH RUSSELL.

Crewel work woman's pocket initialed "S B". Embroidered in wool, on linen, using cross, chain and romanian stitches. The colors used are pink, green, yellow, and blue. 15" $\times$ $12\frac{1}{2}$". THE AUTHOR.

A picture is marked: "Sarah Hampton Anno Dominy 1775" in cross stitch using pink wool. Usually the names and dates are wrought in black. [p.94] In the center there is a large two-handled vase with flowers. This Bucks County girl embroidered different varieties of flowers growing from one stem, reminiscent of the Tree of Life designs. At the bottom of the picture are flowers growing from two mounds and at the top are scattered floral motifs. The picture is worked on a linen ground and is the earliest dated Pennsylvania crewel work picture found thus far.

A crewel work pocket is initialed "S B". [p. 92] The design of vines, roses, tulips and other flowers are worked in chain and romanian stitches. The initials are wrought in cross stitch. Around the edge of the pocket is a chintz border. A number of other crewel pockets have survived.

Crewel work wall pocket initialed "M G" for Mary Gregg, of Chester County. Embroidered in wool, on wool, using cross, stem, bullion knot and long and short stitches. The colors used are pink, red, yellow and blue. 11″ × 8¼″. CHESTER COUNTY HISTORICAL SOCIETY.

Crewel work picture inscribed: "Sarah Hampton Anno Dominy 1775". Embroidered in wool, on linen, using cross, chain, stem, bullion knot, seeding, flat and satin stitches. The colors used are red, pink, blue, yellow and green. 12½" × 17½". CHESTER COUNTY HISTORICAL SOCIETY.

The wall pocket embroidered in wool on a wool ground is initialed "M G" for Mary Gregg of Kennett Township, Chester County. [p. 93] This pocket, having a loop at the top, hung on the wall, and was probably used to hold an almanac. In a farming community an almanac was of the greatest importance. As is frequently found, the centers of the flowers were worked in bullion knots. The petals of the flowers, leaves and stems were wrought in stem and long and short stitches.

Three crewel work pictures are of particular interest. They are so similar in arrangement of motifs and the way that flowers, birds and insects are depicted that one is led to believe that one teacher taught the girls. The earliest picture was embroidered by Elizabeth Jefferis, of Chester County, in 1777. [below] The use of hillocks, at the bottom of the picture, in the English tradition, has been encountered only in this one picture. Flowers grow on the hillocks but there are no prancing animals as might be found in

1777 crewel work picture of Elizabeth Jefferis, of Chester County. Embroidered in wool, on linen, using cross, bullion knot, stem, seeding, satin, long and short, fishbone and chain stitches. The colors used are red, pink, green, blue, yellow, brown, gray, lavender, rust and white. $34'' \times 31\frac{5}{8}''$. THE METROPOLITAN MUSEUM OF ART.

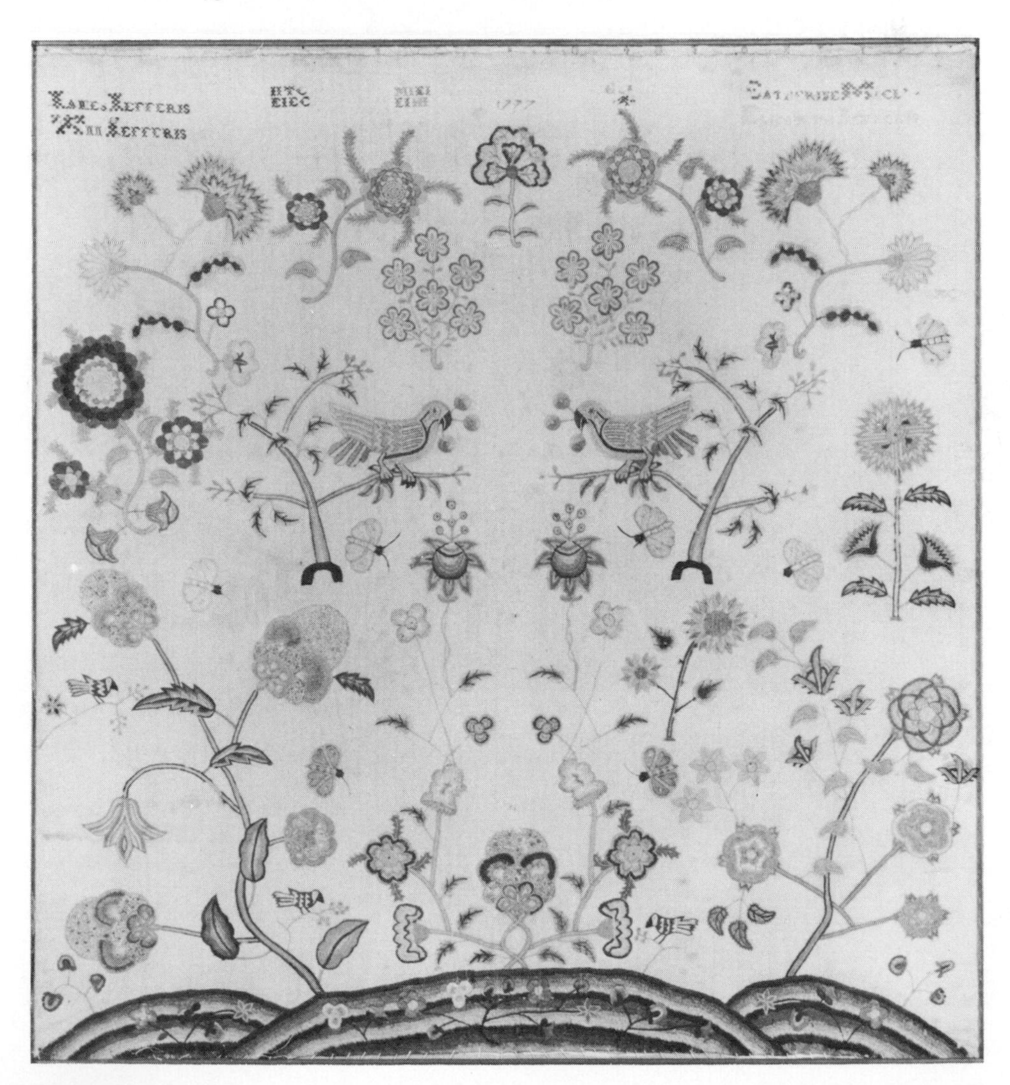

English Jacobean crewel. Two parrots with cherries in their beaks perch on small trees, and scattered throughout the picture are other small birds and butterflies. The hillocks, flowers, leaves, birds and butterflies are surprisingly solidly worked. When regarded closely the design is not continuous, as in the English Jacobean crewel work. Instead, it has small scattered motifs in the American tradition. This picture is executed in cross, bullion knot, stem, speckling, satin, long and short, fishbone and chain stitches in wool on a linen ground. No other piece of crewel work has been found in Pennsylvania in which so many different stitches were employed.

The second picture was worked by Sarah Smedley, of Chester County, in 1788 in wool on linen.[2] She wrought a mere suggestion of three hillocks, the same two parrots sit on trees with three cherries in their beaks and there are two butterflies. Sarah Smedley's picture is simpler in design than Elizabeth Jefferis's and does not include the small birds or as many small scattered floral motives. In the center she added a basket of stiffly growing flowers.

The latest of the three similar pictures is initialed and dated "E G 1791" and "R H 1764". [plate III] The three hillocks are suggested by a few lines of stem stitches. The parrots, with berries in their beaks, perching on trees, are almost as large as the trees. At this time Carolina paroquets were still living in Pennsylvania and a parrot with a cherry in its beak is thought to symbolize wealth and plenty. In all three pictures roses, carnations, tulips and other flowers grow from the same stems, reminiscent of the Jacobean Tree of Life designs except on a much smaller scale. A few silk threads have been used sparingly to add life and luster to this picture.

The Pennsylvania designs for crewel work taken from nature were simpler than their English prototypes and were worked in the simpler stitches in bright colors. Many of the women in the country must have made their own designs, having first washed, carded, spun and dyed the wool.

1791 crewel work picture initialed "E G". Embroidered in wool and silk, on using stem, satin, bullion knot, cross and long and short stitches. 33½″ × 28″. THE AUTHOR.

SILK EMBROIDERY

BEGINNING in the eighteenth century silk was used for many of the most important pieces of Pennsylvania needlework. Using silk made a greater delicacy of line possible in addition to an improvement in shading techniques. Embroidery in silk, on a satin or silk ground, is a more difficult type of needlework than embroidery in wool on a linen or canvas ground. With silk the direction of the stitches is of the utmost importance as is the necessity of having a smooth even surface to the finished embroidery. It is necessary to work silk embroidery in a frame.

Silk is thought to have been used by the Chinese two thousand and seven hundred years before the Christian era. It was not known in Europe until the sixth century when monks successfully smuggled some of the precious silkworms out of China. The manufacture reached France during the reign of Charles VIII and it was introduced into England during the first part of the fifteenth century.

It is possible that some of the embroidery silk used in Pennsylvania was of American manufacture. During the eighteenth and nineteenth centuries Americans had attempted to grow mulberry trees in order to feed the silkworms mulberry leaves. In Pennsylvania as early as 1725 James Logan, secretary to William Penn, wrote "The culture of silk in this country is extremely beneficial and promising."[1] The Moravians, at Bethlehem, planted the European white mulberry trees and made silk for a while, but this attempt as well as the similar attempts by other religious groups were not successful. The tedious hours of hand operations were not practical in America where labor was scarce and for that reason valuable.

Benjamin Franklin, agent of the colony in Great Britain, sought to establish silk culture in Pennsylvania. About 1765 he sent silkworm eggs and mulberry cuttings to Pennsylvania and on January 5, 1770, he wrote to the American Philosophical Society urging it to encourage silk culture. On February 2, 1770, the Society presented a petition to the General Assembly: "That a public filature be established at Philadelphia and afterwards at other places in the Province . . . for winding Cocoons . . . That to encourage all Persons to cultivate Mulberry trees, raise Silk worms and bring their Cocoons to the filature . . . a sum of not less than £500 p. annum should be appropriated during the aforesaid term of five years."[2] The Assembly failed to make the proposed appropriation.

Before the Revolution some silk was produced in various parts of the state, particularly in Lancaster County. In 1770 Susanna Wright of Columbia made a piece of mantina sixty yards long from silk from her cocoons; this cloth was worn as a court dress by the Queen of England. Silk culture in Pennsylvania terminated for a time with the Revolution.

In 1826 there was renewed enthusiasm for raising silk because of the introduction of *Morus multicaulis,* a superior species of mulberry tree for silk culture. The newspapers were full of accounts of fortunes made. Thousands of acres of mulberry trees were planted. At Newtown and Doylestown, Bucks County, buildings were erected especially to rear silkworms. Philadelphia was a center of the craze. Peter S. Dupoceau of Philadelphia established a "School of Filature" for teaching the delicate art of reeling silk from cocoons and in 1837 The Philadelphia Silk Culture and Manufacturing Company was established.

Picture worked by Ann Marsh. Embroidered in silk and metallic threads, on satin, using French knot and long and short stitches. The colors used are blue, yellow, green, tan and gold. 7½″ × 8½″. CHESTER COUNTY HISTORICAL SOCIETY.

Pincushion made by Ann Marsh. Embroidered in silk, on canvas, using petit point, French knot and brick stitches. The colors used are green, yellow, purple, red and blue. 5″ × 3¼″. CHESTER COUNTY HISTORICAL SOCIETY.

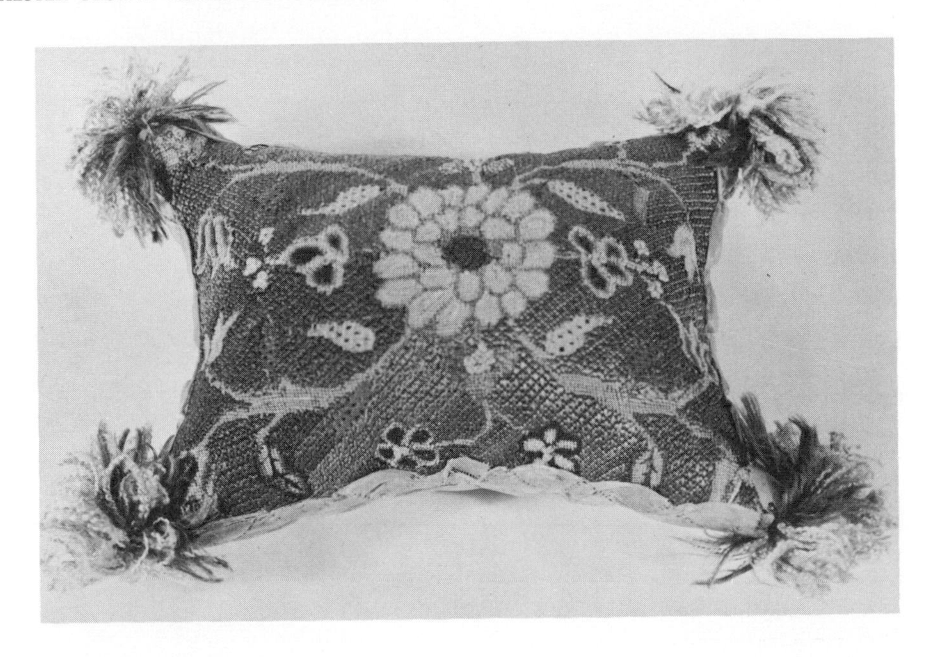

Two years later the bubble burst. It developed that the *multicaulis* trees could not withstand the Pennsylvania winters. Thousands of trees died and fortunes were lost.

In Philadelphia the newspapers carried advertisements of both men and women announcing that they taught embroidery and painting on silks and satins during the eighteenth century. In 1759:

> Mrs. Whitby from London now living at Daniel Hoots, next door to Roberts Coffee House, teaches all sorts of embroidery in gold, silver, silk or worsted. Bugel or Snail work, also to pickel, preserve and make fine Paste, likewise dry'd gravies from the sea.[3]

In 1768:

> Barnard Andrews, Embroiderer and Box maker, in Sixth street, three doors above Market street; Works, mends and cleans all sorts of embroidery in the newest and neatest fashion, such as any kind of cloaths, for gentlemen and ladies, pulpit cloths, &c. either in gold, silver or silk, with all sorts of tassels for the same . . .
>
> If there are any ladies that have an inclination to learn embroidery or any of the above-mentioned work, he will either attend them at his own or their houses, as it shall best suit those who please to employ him.[4]

In 1775:

> Sarah Hussey. Tambour Worker and Embroiderer, in Second street, between Chestnut and Walnut streets, at the house lately occupied by M'Elroy and Finley, nearly opposite to the Golden Fleece; where she teaches Ladies the Tambour and Embroidery in gold and silver, sheneal silk and cotton; the open work in the muslins and elegance in shading; to spangle and pearl, &c. for Twenty Shillings per month. Ladies may be taught at their own houses for the same. She returns her sincere thanks to those Ladies that have experienced her judgement in shading and hopes for their recommendations. Ladies gowns, ruffles, aprons, work bags and fire screens worked very cheap; also shoes worked in Gold, for one dollar a pair. Likewise Gentlemens mourning cloaths embroidered, and waistcoats worked in Tambour, from

3 l to 10 l in gold, and without from 3 l to 15s. hat bands, buttons and loops, and buttons for Gentlemens cloaths embroidered with gold and silver, to any design that they chuse.[5]

In 1790 James Cox advertised:

Drawing & Painting . . . that he has removed his School opposite to Mr. John Elliott's the Bank side of Front street, below Chestnut street—Where he continues Instructing Youth in the useful and elegant Accom-

1752 picture by Sarah Wistar, of Philadelphia. Embroidered in silk, using satin, French knot and long and short stitches. The colors used are red, cream, blue, yellow, green, brown and tan. $9\frac{1}{2}'' \times 7''$. COURTESY HENRY FRANCIS DUPONT WINTERTHUR MUSEUM.

> plishments of Drawing and Painting, upon Paper, Glass, Muslin, and Sattin; also; Shading with India Ink . . .
>
> Copperplate Prints, Maps and Paintings, accurately copied; Drawing and Shading on Sattin for Needle-work; . . .[6]

In 1793 Samuel Folwell advertised:

> A Drawing-School for Young Ladies . . . as also painting upon sattin, ivory or paper[7]

The painting on materials advertised by James Cox and Samuel Folwell would have been used by the girls for the backgrounds, hands and faces of the silk embroidered pictures.

In 1752 Sarah Wistar, of Philadelphia, embroidered in silk on silk two small pictures of birds perched in flowering trees. The mounds with a rabbit are similar to those found in English crewel work. It is probably that the parrot was copied from a design book as its feet are near but not holding onto the branch on which it is supposedly perched. [p. 101]

A pincushion and a picture were embroidered by Ann Marsh. [p. 99] The pincushion is worked on a canvas ground using silk thread. The leaves and petals of the flowers are worked in petit point stitches, the centers of the flowers in French knots. The background is wrought in brick stitch. The four tassels are made from the same colored silks as used in the needlework.

The picture initialed "A M" is wrought on a silk ground using both silk and metallic threads. [p. 99] The petals of the flowers, two-handled urn and some of the stems are outlined with metallic threads that have been couched down. Except for the centers of the flowers which are worked with French knots, the picture is wrought using the long and short stitch. Other similar pictures are known to have been made by Ann Marsh.

Biblical and historical subjects were embroidered in silk as pictures during the eighteenth and part of the nineteenth centuries. [p. 114] Many of them were copies of paintings or prints. Those worked in silk on a satin or silk ground usually had the faces and hands of the people and the sky painted on the ground either by a professional artist or by the embroideress herself. The remaining sections of the pictures were worked in silk or sometimes in a combination of silk and chenille threads. Infrequently metallic threads and sequins were employed to add luster.

By family tradition the picture of Lady Jane Grey was worked by a member of the Juvenal family at a Female Academy, in Philadel-

Picture attributed to a member of the Juvenal family, of Philadelphia. Embroidered in silk and chenille, on silk, using satin, long and short and feather stitches. The colors used are brown, red, blue, gray, rose, tan, cream, yellow, gold and white. The sky, faces and hands are painted on the satin. Metallic threads and sequins were used for decoration. 35½″ × 27½″. MRS. J. RAMSEY VAN RODEN AND HOWELL BARRETT PENNELL.

phia, about mid-eighteenth century. [p. 103] Legend relates that the faces were painted by Benjamin West on the silk ground before the picture was embroidered. The sky, faces and hands are painted. The remaining portions are worked in fine silk, a crinkled silk and chenille threads thus giving perspective to the picture. Metallic thread was employed for the ropes and tassels, and sequins for trim on the people's clothes and again on the draperies. The gold leaf frame is original. This picture is beautifully executed. The topic must have been a very popular one during the eighteenth century. A number of other similar pictures are known.

Mourning pictures were popular subjects for needlework from the end of the eighteenth century until about 1840 when Berlin work gained the attention of the women. They were especially popular at the time that George Washington died in 1799. Many of the embroideries either mention his name or have his portrait on the urn and some include both. The mourning picture of Margaret Seeger has an applied printed portrait of Washington on the urn and painted on the silk ground is the inscription: "THY LOSS EVER SHALL WE MOURN. SACRED TO THE MEMORY OF THE ILLUSTRIOUS WASHINGTON". [plate IV] The sky and part of the urn are painted on the ground and the remaining portions of the picture are embroidered in silk. Much symbolism is expressed, such as the reversed musket, the weeping woman and the weeping willow tree, the urn and the black drape on Liberty. Liberty acquired a particular importance because it symbolized the American dream. The eagle with the olive branch in its claws represents America and Peace. The cap on the staff represents Liberty. The Liberty cap derives its name from the old Roman tradition that a freed slave was permitted to wear a blue cap as a symbol of freedom. It is thought that the fad for making these memorial pictures sprang from the teachings of the Moravian sect.

MORAVIAN NEEDLEWORK

THE Church of the United Brethren, commonly called Moravians, has distinguished itself particularly in the work of its missions and in the cause of education. In December, 1741, Nicholas Lewis, Count of Zinzendorf, arrived in Pennsylvania accompanied by a small group of followers, one of whom was his daughter, Benigna. On May 4, 1742, Benigna, assisted by two women and three men, opened a school in the Ashmead House in Germantown with twenty-five pupils. This school was the actual beginning of the educational work of the Moravian Church in Pennsylvania. In less than two months the school was transferred from Germantown to Bethlehem, the town intended to be the spiritual center of all Moravians in the New World. On May 8, 1745, the pupils were moved to the "Whitefield House" in Nazareth and on January 6, 1749, they were returned to Bethlehem.

In the diary of the church for that day is found:

> In the afternoon the children arrived from Nazareth who are henceforth to constitute our little boarding-school for girls here. There are sixteen of them, together with the Sisters who are to have charge of them, and they moved into the rooms newly added to the house hitherto occupied by married men and women and with beautiful music and a pleasant love-feast.[1]

From this date the Bethlehem Boarding School's undisturbed local history begins. In 1899 Bishop J. Mortimer Levering stated:

> . . . in those early days it was a privilege highly prized to have a daughter under such care and training, taken from the remote backwoods homes in many cases and brought in contact with gentle, pious women of refinement; and while in many things they had to conform to a very plain way of life and to join in various kinds of manual labor, they were taught not merely reading and writing in English and German, arithmetic and geography, something of history in evening talks, something of botany on their rambles around Bethlehem, but also plain and fancy needlework and vocal and instrumental music.[2]

One of the earliest surviving pieces of embroidery made in Bethlehem was a banner worked in 1778 by the single Sisters commemorating the gallantry of Count Casimir Pulaski. He had been instrumental in maintaining a cordial relationship between the American army and the local inhabitants of Bethlehem. The army used the choir-houses as barracks, hospitals and guard houses for the English prisoners. On one side of the banner "U S" is embroidered encircled by the motto "Unitas virtus fortior"; on the other side is embroidered the all-seeing eye of God, in the midst of the thirteen stars of the Union, surrounded by the words "Non alius regit". The designs are embroidered with yellow silk, the letters shaded with green. A deep green bullion fringe ornaments the edges.[3]

In 1787 the Bethlehem Boarding School was charging seventeen shillings sixpence per quarter for tambour work and drawing.[4]

"Daddy Thomas", employed at the school between 1788 and 1813 and a favorite of the pupils, is reported to have said: "How well you look today young ladies!—all pictures of health! And here is your beautiful needlework! You can make the strawberries but can't eat them!"[5]

From a journal kept by the younger pupils of the school we

learn how the days were spent: "Oct. 22. 1788.—At eight A.M., Mr. Hubener kept our arithmetical school. At nine we had English grammar, in which he assisted us. At eleven, we attended English children's meeting. At one P.M., there was tambour and music, and at three, we went to walk. At half-past seven, there was the evening meeting."[6] "Nov 25.—Dr. Attwood, of New York, brought his daughter to school. Several of the children played on the spinet for them, which they appeared to like very much. We also showed them our needlework."[7] In 1791, "April 9.—In the morning we were making preparations for the love-feast. In the afternoon, at two o'clock, we assembled in the hall to conclude our examination by a love-feast, during which were shown to the company specimens of our writing, drawing, painting, embroidery, and tambour, and of the younger misses' knitting and samplers."[8]

In 1790 a circular of the school mentioned the charge "For instruction in fine needlework, including drawing, also two guineas per year." Tambour work continued a favorite mode of embroidery.[9]

In May, 1807, instruction in artificial flowers, a new branch of fancy needlework, was given at a charge of £ 1 13s 9d per quarter. During the winter of 1816–1817 social evenings in the principal's room were attended by the older pupils in turn. Sometimes a book was read aloud by one of the company while the rest were busied with ornamental works of skill. Specimens of crepe and ribbon work had been brought from Germany to Bethlehem which had been greatly admired. In 1818 instruction in this type of embroidery was given by Sister Polly Blum. Crepe and ribbon work remained popular for upwards of twenty years.[10]

In 1826 the pupils, under the direction of Sister Blum, worked an elaborate embroidery in ribbon and silk for the wife of President Adams.[11] In 1835 it was mentioned that needlework was engaged in by a larger number of the pupils than at any previous time[12] and as late as 1860 a charge was made for extra studies not included in

1811 pastoral picture of Catharine Kapp, Lititz. Embroidered in silk and chenille, on satin, using satin, French knot and stem stitches. Much of the picture is painted on the satin. The colors used are yellow, gold, blue, green, brown and white. 16½″ × 17″. LINDEN HALL SCHOOL.

general tuition: "Ornamental Needlework, in Worsted, Chenille, etc., for 50 lessons $3.00."[13]

The second oldest Moravian school dates back to 1746, when the Moravians broke ground in Warwick Township, Lancaster County, for the Gemeinhaus: a log building which served as chapel, schoolhouse and parsonage. The school commenced with an enrollment of four boys and three girls with the Reverend Leonard Schnell and his wife as the first teachers. In 1766 the school was moved to Lititz. There the girls were taught in the Sisters' House, which later became Linden Hall Seminary.

Between 1800 and 1802 Sister Rosel Beyer taught sewing, knitting and darning. Among the other teachers was Sister Polly

Heckwelder, daughter of the well-known Indian missionary and pioneer of the western frontier. She taught ornamental needlework, for which the school was famous.[14]

On April 18, 1801 Sister Penny wrote:

> Last week our children had their examination and many from Lancaster who had girls in our boarding school came here to see and hear what

1819 tribute of gratitude from the pupils of Lititz Academy to the Reverend Andrew Benade. Embroidered in silk and chenille, on satin, using satin, French knot, long and short and stem stitches. The colors used are red, yellow, green, brown, blue, gray, gold, black and white. 23″ × 21″. LINDEN HALL SCHOOL.

improvement their children had made. They were examined in spelling, reading, and writing, German and English, arithmetic, grammar, geography, music, knitting, tambour and embroidery or satin stitch as I believe you call it more properly.[15]

1835 floral picture of Lisetta M. Ham, Lititz. Embroidered in ribbon, crepe, silk and chenille, on satin, using stem, French knot and satin stitches. $23\frac{1}{2}'' \times 20''$. LINDEN HALL SCHOOL.

Besides teaching needlework the Sisters also did sewing, knitting, embroidering and weaving as a means of livelihood.

During the nineteenth century various types of floral embroidery in colored silks, ribbon and crepe needlework, pictorial embroidery worked in silk on a silk or satin background, and mourning pictures worked in silk on the same backgrounds became known as Bethlehem or Moravian embroidery. This was the romantic period in needlework. Typical of the period is the pastoral scene worked by Catharine Kapp, "Litaz", in 1811. [p. 108] A shepherdess with a lamb in her lap rests under a tree, while in the background there is a pond, a summer house and a small cottage with smoke coming from the chimney. The picture is embroidered, using both silk and chenille thread. The head and arms of the woman, pond, sky and a few of the leaves at the side of the pond are painted on the silk background. The stitches used are outline, French knots and satin. Surrounding the rural scene is a garland of flowers tied with a chenille bow.

One of the rarest and finest examples of Lititz School needlework is the tribute from the pupils to Andrew Benade. [p. 109] In the center of the picture is a monument with a woman at the right, a tree at either side and the school itself in the background. The monument is inscribed:

50
Febr 20th 1819
The Blessing of the
LORD
be upon

YOU!
We bless YOU in the
Name of the
LORD!

Vase with flowers. Embroidered in silk, chenille and ribbon on satin. The colors used are green, brown, yellow, pink and red. 21″ × 17″. MORAVIAN MUSEUM OF BETHLEHEM.

In the lower left hand corner is a book inscribed: "To the Reverend ANDREW BENADE—a tribute of GRATITUDE from the Pupils of LITIZ ACADEMY Feb 20th 1819". The sky, school in

Mourning picture made by Margaret Seeger, of Lancaster County. Embroidered in silk, on silk, using flat stitches. The sky, faces, hands and inscriptions on urn are painted on the satin. $23\frac{1}{2}'' \times 20''$. THE AUTHOR.

the distance, urn, book on the urn, stream of water, face of the book in the foreground, face, hands, headdress of the woman and the bush behind her are painted on the satin. The weeping willow leaves, the dress and scarf on the woman, the cross, the garland on the urn and the flowers in the narrow border are worked in silk thread. The trunk of the willow tree, rocks, bushes both sides of the urn, the tree on the right and the ground are embroidered in chenille. Two rows of tinsel thread surround the floral border and sequins were used, as trim, on the woman's dress.

Floral embroidery was the usual form of practice for the pupils. The wreath of flowers, with a basket of flowers, in the center is marked: "Lisetta M. Ham. Litiz June 20th 1835." [p. 110] Some of the flowers are made of ribbon and some are made of crepe. Most of the leaves and small tendrils are worked on the satin background, using either silk or chenille thread. In the wreath of flowers is inscribed: "Margaret Hummel, Litiz Seminary December 29, 1837."[16] Some of the crepe flowers stand out from the background material about an inch. Each petal of the roses has been laid petal on petal to build up to the whole flower. Many of the buds and centers of the crepe flowers are made of ribbon. Some of the leaves and the tendrils are worked on the satin background, using chenille and silk thread. The predominant colors are green, rose, yellow, blue and brown. Because of the excellence of execution the vase of flowers, embroidered with silk, chenille and ribbon on a satin background would have been a pupil's master piece. [p. 112]

Mourning pictures were a popular subject with the Moravians. That worked by Maria Eichler to the "MEMORY OF MY DEAR UNCLE AND AUNT GEORGE AND ANNA S NEIDLER." is an excellent example.[17] In the center is the ever-present monument surmounted with an urn, overhung by the branches of a weeping willow tree. Standing at the side of the urn is a weeping female figure. In this instance she carries a basket of flowers. The woman's hands and face are painted on the satin background. Sometimes the faces were painted on cardboard and then attached to the background while at other times the hair of the departed was used in the picture. The inscription on the urn is in india ink. The roses

Biblical picture. Embroidered in silk and chenille, on satin, using long and short, French knot and satin stitches. The sky, hill, faces, hands, hair and feet are painted. The colors used are green, brown, gold and red. 34½″ × 28½″. ANNIE S. KEMERER MUSEUM.

Isaac & Rebekah. Embroidered in silk and chenille, on satin, using long and short and satin stitches. The hands, legs, faces, sky and man on the far left are painted. Metallic thread was used to trim the dress of the woman in the center. The colors used are blue, brown, pink, gold, gray, black and white. 17″ × 33″, WHITEFIELD HOUSE MUSEUM, MORAVIAN HISTORICAL SOCIETY.

are made of crepe, the woman's dress and the flowers in her basket are worked in silk thread, the sky is painted and the remainder of the picture is embroidered with chenille thread.

Biblical subjects were also embroidered in the Moravian schools and by the Sisters. The picture of the Ascension of Christ [p. 114] embroidered in silk and chenille thread on a satin background was probably copied from a contemporary print. The sky, hill and heads, hands and feet of the people are painted on the satin. The building, clothing of the people, wings of the angels and faces of the lambs are embroidered in silk while the remainder has been

Biblical picture. Embroidered in wool, silk and chenille, on canvas, in cross stitch. The colors used are green, blue, red, orange, pink, brown, yellow and black. $20\frac{1}{4}'' \times 17\frac{3}{4}''$. ANNIE S. KEMERER MUSEUM.

worked in chenille. As has been frequently found on the silk embroidered pictures few stitches are employed. The picture of "Isaac & Rebekah" [p. 115] is also worked in silk and chenille thread on a satin background. As is found on the other pictorial embroidery the faces, hands and sky are painted on the satin. The dress of the main woman is interesting as it has been trimmed with a tinsel edging.

Biblical subjects were also worked on a canvas background. The picture of the women and children visiting Christ was embroidered in cross stitch using wool, silk and chenille threads. It is unusually colorful, having been embroidered in shades of green, blue, red, orange, pink, brown, yellow and black. [p. 116]

Crewel work was also done by the Sisters. The pocket, finely worked in chain stitch, was made in the Sisters' House in Nazareth about 1800. [p. 118] Shades of red, blue, yellow, pink, gold,

Communion cloth found in the Sisters' House, in Lititz. Embroidered in red wool, on cotton in satin stitch. The inscription, translated into English, reads: "May our souls be blessed on this day of grace, and our bodies likewise participate. May the blood that flowed from this wound refresh us and Thy body become our Redeemer." 30½" × 30". WHITEFIELD HOUSE MUSEUM, MORAVIAN HISTORICAL SOCIETY.

Crewel pocket worked in the Sisters' House, in Nazareth, circa 1800. Embroidered in wool, on linen, using the chain stitch. The colors used are red, blue, yellow, pink, gold, green and white. 13″ × 9½″. WHITEFIELD MUSEUM HOUSE, MORAVIAN HISTORICAL SOCIETY.

Bead collar, made in the Sisters' House, in Lititz, in 1837. JOHANNES MUELLER HOUSE.

Child's dress, worn by Sister Louise Kummer, circa 1800. Embroidered in wool, on cotton, in chain stitch. The colors used are red, green and gold. WHITEFIELD MUSEUM HOUSE, MORAVIAN HISTORICAL SOCIETY.

LEFT. Bead work woman's bag and bead work border for a dress. Pink, red, blue, yellow, green, gold, orange and black beads were used. RIGHT. Woman's bag embroidered in silk and chenille, on satin, using stem, French knot and satin stitches. Many of the flowers are made of ribbon. MORAVIAN MUSEUM OF BETHLEHEM.

Child's cotton dress and knitted bonnet embroidered with beads. Pink, red, blue, yellow, black and white beads were used. MORAVIAN MUSEUM OF BETHLEHEM.

1833 sampler showing the "Litiz" Seminary marked; "Worked by Rebecca G McCord in the 11 year of her age 1822". Embroidered in silk, on linen, using satin, cross, double cross, eyelet and rococo stitches. The colors used are blue, green, brown, yellow, lavender and black 22″ × 13″. LINDEN HALL SCHOOL.

green and white are well balanced in the design. The child's dress, worn by Sister Louise Kummer, about 1815 [p. 118] is also embroidered in chain stitch. The leaves are different shades of green. The borders around the sleeves and the bottom of the dress are worked in shades of green, gold and red. As in the pocket, the chain stitch is beautifully executed. The communion cloth, [p. 117] embroidered in red wool on a cotton background, in satin stitch, was found in the Sisters' House in Lititz. The translation of the German is "May our souls be blessed on this day of grace, and our bodies likewise participate. May the blood that flowed from this wound refresh us and Thy body become our Redeemer."

The sampler worked by Rebecca G. McCord, in 1833, at the age of eleven years, at Lititz School [p. 120] included five alphabets, three sets of numerals, the initials of other members of her family, floral motifs and the "Litiz seminary" building. Enclosed in the yard of the school are two small black dogs thought to have belonged to the headmistress. The sampler was worked on coarse linen, using satin, cross, eyelet and rococco stitches. Samplers showing the school building are extremely rare.

Bead work was another accomplishment of the Sisters at Bethlehem, Nazareth and Lititz. The bead collar was made in the Sisters' House, in Lititz, in 1837. [p. 118] The child's cotton dress [p. 119] has a bead flower and leaves on the bodice and a border of flowers and leaves around the bottom. The child's knitted cap has beads knitted in the design. Women's bags and borders for dresses [p. 119] were also embroidered with beads. The colors of the beads used by the Moravians on the examples of beadwork mentioned are pink, red, blue, yellow, green, gold, orange, black and white.

FLORENTINE EMBROIDERY

FLORENTINE embroidery is variously known as "bargello," "Irish," "fiammá" and "point d'hongrie." Legend has it that a Hungarian bride of a Medici brought this work with her to Florence, Italy, in the fifteenth century. Basically it is a straight gobelin stitch worked in a symmetrical pattern on a canvas ground over a random number of threads. The name "flame stitch" is most descriptive, since the usual zigzag lines bear a resemblance to flames of fire. The feature of this needlework is the effective shading and blending of the colors in wool or silk thread. Florentine stitch was used in Pennsylvania frequently in the second half of the eighteenth century. Bible covers, chair seats, men's and women's pocketbooks or purses, needlecases, pot holders, eye-glass cases and pincushions have been found embroidered in this stitch.

Book bindings entirely of needlework began to be embroidered and appreciated in England and Germany at the end of the sixteenth century. In England they remained popular until about the end of the seventeenth century and were frequently wrought in petit point, tent, cross, pearl and raised embroidery. In Pennsylvania four family Bibles are known that have embroidered covers worked in Florentine stitch.

The cover for the 1723 Morris family Bible, published in

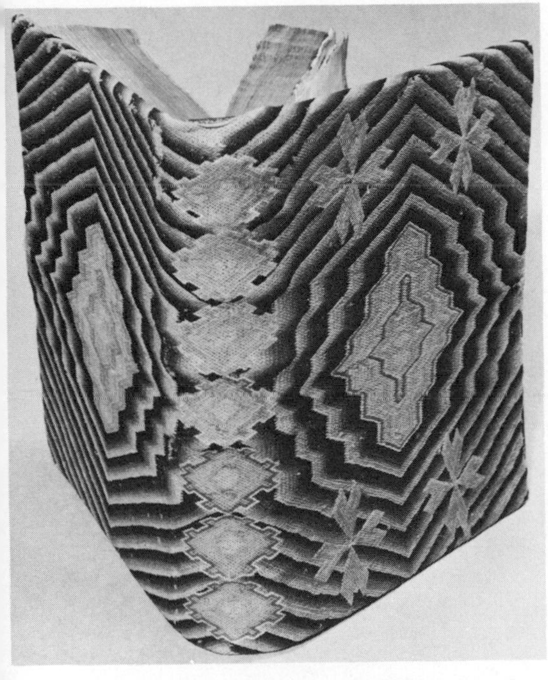

ABOVE. Bible cover worked in Florentine stitch, in wool, on a canvas ground. The Bible was published in 1760 and the needlework is dated 1765. The cover was probably made by Ann Flower who married Samuel Wheeler. The colors used are green and pink. H. 8″, W. 5″.
MR. & MRS. SAMUEL W. MORRIS.

LEFT. Bible cover worked in Florentine stitch, in wool, on a canvas ground. Inside the 1723 London Bible is inscribed: "Deborah Morris Her Book" and "The Gift of Anthony Morris Jun to his Son Samuel Morris Jun in June 1756 and through Catharine W Morris to Israel W Morris in 12th Month 1859". The colors used are green, yellow and red. H. 14″, W. 9½″, spine 2¾″.
MR. & MRS. SAMUEL W. MORRIS.

London, has the most elaborate Florentine stitch pattern found as a book cover. [above, left] Thirteen medallions are surrounded by the usual zigzag lines worked in graduated shades of green, red and yellow. The cover of the Wheeler family Bible has a simpler design worked in shades of green and pink. [above, right] The cover may have been made by Ann Flower, daughter of Enoch, who was one

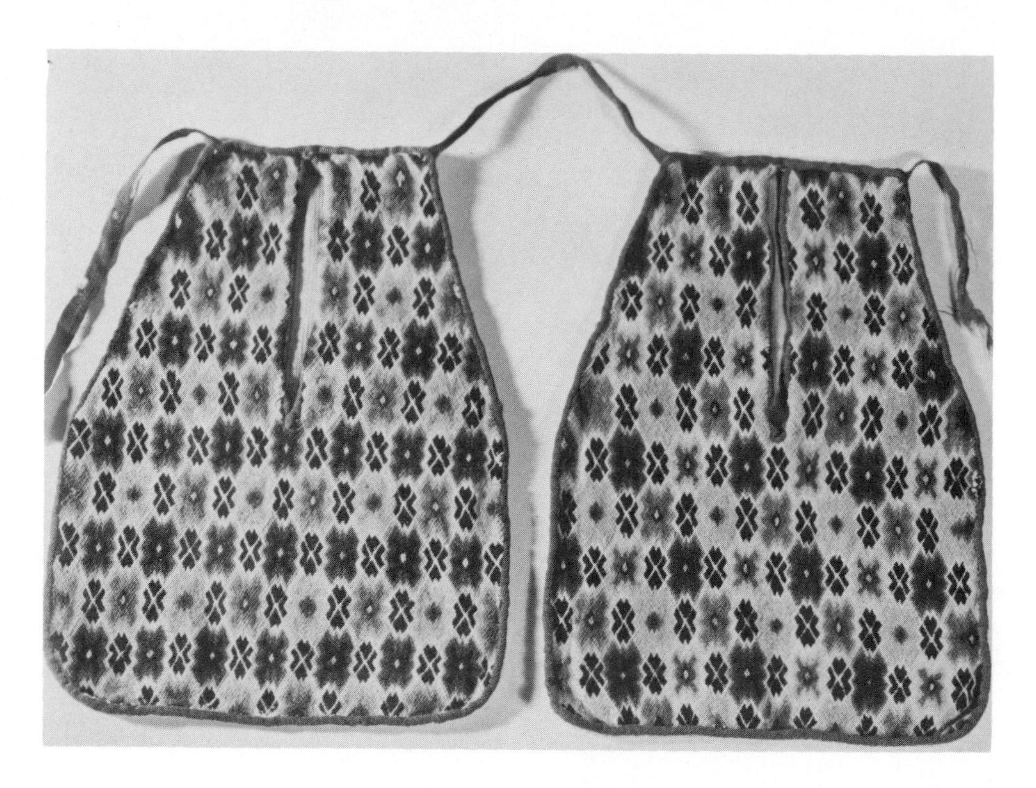

Woman's pockets worked in Florentine stitch, in wool, on a canvas ground. Pockets were worn under the outer skirt to hold the articles that a woman would need. The colors used are yellow, green, blue, red and black. 13¼″ × 5¾″ to 10″. CHESTER COUNTY HISTORICAL SOCIETY.

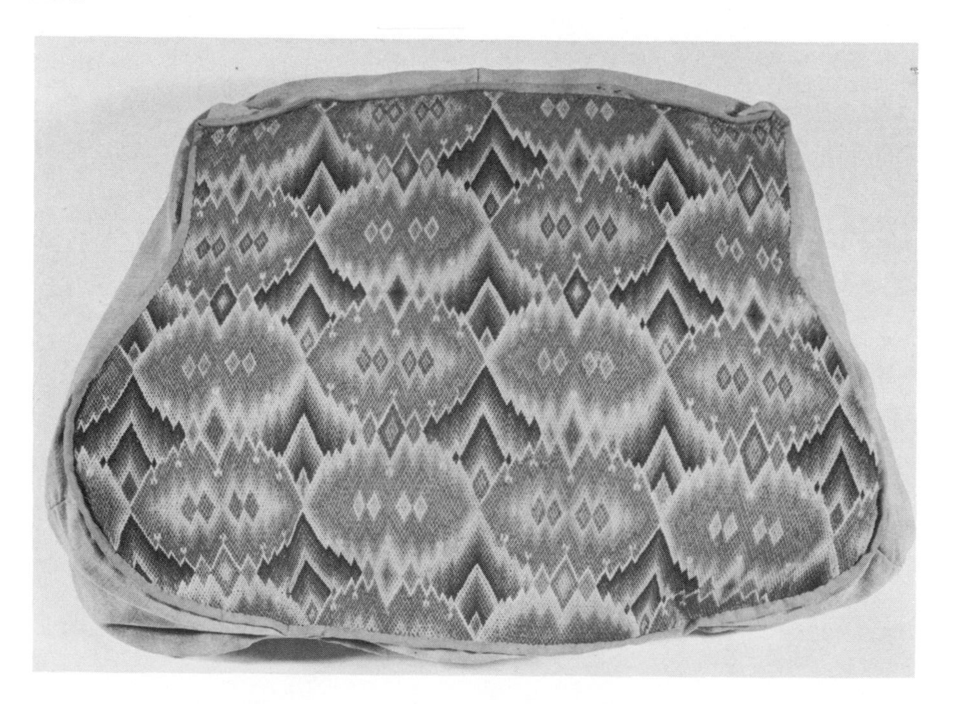

Cushion worked by Ann Marsh in Florentine stitch, in wool, on a canvas ground. The colors used are blue, green, pink and yellow. 22″ × 17½″. CHESTER COUNTY HISTORICAL SOCIETY.

of the first school teachers in Philadelphia. She married Samuel Wheeler.

The Bible of John Gillingham, cabinetmaker in Philadelphia, cost four pounds and ten shillings. It is inscribed: "John Gillingham

Man's pocket-book initialed and dated "I T 1777" for Joseph Taylor, of Chester County. It is worked in Florentine stitch, in wool, on a canvas ground. The colors used are pink, rust, blue, green and black. Closed 4″ × 7″. CHESTER COUNTY HISTORICAL SOCIETY.

Pot holder and purse worked in Florentine stitch, in wool, on a canvas ground. The pot holder is worked in yellow, blue, rust and green. $6\frac{3}{4}$″ × $6\frac{1}{2}$″ at largest sections. The purse is worked in yellow, lavender, green and pink. $3\frac{3}{4}$″ × $4\frac{1}{4}$″. CHESTER COUNTY HISTORICAL SOCIETY.

His Bible, Bought of Benjamin Franklin May 20, 1740." The Florentine stitch cover was probably made by his wife Ann. John Gillingham died during the yellow fever epidemic in 1793. His inventory, taken the following year, lists "One Family Bible 1 10 0."[1]

The Florentine stitch cushion embroidered by Ann Marsh, an English girl who came to Pennsylvania and taught school in Philadelphia, was worked in shades of pink, blue and green. [p. 124] The diamond pattern used for this cushion is frequently found on examples of Florentine embroidery in this area. Another seat cover is marked "L P 1763" for Lydia Painter, of Chester County. The cover is of brilliant color, having been worked in shades of pink, blue, green, yellow, brown, rust, black and white. [plate IV]

Many men's pocket-books were embroidered in Florentine stitch and frequently initialed and dated. The pocket-book marked "I T 1777" was made for Joseph Taylor, of Chester County. [p. 125] The shading is from pink to rust and blue to green. Known examples of Pennsylvania pocket-books date from 1750 to 1799. A tape was usually attached to tie them.

Needle-cases and pincushions were also executed in Florentine stitch. The needle-case initialed and dated "M D 1766" was embroidered with Florentine stitch on the outside and crewel work on the inside, a rare combination. [p. 91] The colors yellow, blue, green, pink, rust and lavender are employed for both the Florentine embroidery and for the crewel work.

The Florentine stitch pot holder is the only one that has been found thus far. It is wrought in shades of yellow, blue, rust and green. The purse is interesting as it is embroidered in silk thread throughout. [p. 125] Another rarity, found in Chester County, is the pair of women's pockets embroidered in shades of yellow, green, blue, red and black. It is the only pair of pockets, found thus far, embroidered in either canvas or crewel embroidery. [p. 124]

CANVAS WORK

CAUFEILD and Saward in the *Dictionary of Needlework* in describing canvas work write: "Before the introduction of Berlin patterns, in 1805, all wool work upon canvas was called by this name, which has now, however, become almost obsolete . . . Ancient Canvas Work was done upon very fine canvas in Tent Stitch, and was really Tapestry Work." The same dictionary defines Berlin Work in part as: "A modern name given to the Opus Pulvinarium of the ancients, and also known as Cushion Style and Point de Marque. Opus Pulvinarium was well known to the Phrygians and Egyptians, and its principal stitch (Cross Stitch) was used in the curtains of the Tabernacle. The work was prevalent during the thirteenth and following centuries, but then chiefly used for kneeling mats and cushions in churches, as it was more durable than embroidery. From this application it owed its name of Cushion style . . . During the fifteenth and sixteenth centuries Tent Stitch was more used than Cross Stitch for this work, and it was called Canvas Work until the present century, when the production of Berlin coloured paper patterns, in 1804, procured for it the title of Berlin Work, though this last name was not finally adopted until 1820, the date of the introduction of Berlin wools, which took the place of the crewels, lambswools, and silks, that had been used up to that period. The patterns worked until the Berlin ones were printed were drawn directly on to the canvas, and the places to be coloured were painted in their various shades, so that but little variety could be marked out, and more was left to individual taste . . ."

Randle Holmes in *The Academy of Armory; or a Display of Heraldry,* published in 1701, shows a picture of a man sitting at a four-legged table, closely resembling today's card table, the top of which is an embroidery frame. He describes the picture in the following manner: "He beareth Argent, or IMBRAUTHERER sowing a piece of work in a Tent, the Table, Or, the Imbrauthery variable

Pincushion initialed and dated "M H 1764" for Martha Hickman, of Chester County. Worked in wool, on canvas, using cross and tent stitches. The colors used are blue, red, yellow, rust, green, natural and black. 10″ × 6½″. CHESTER COUNTY HISTORICAL SOCIETY.

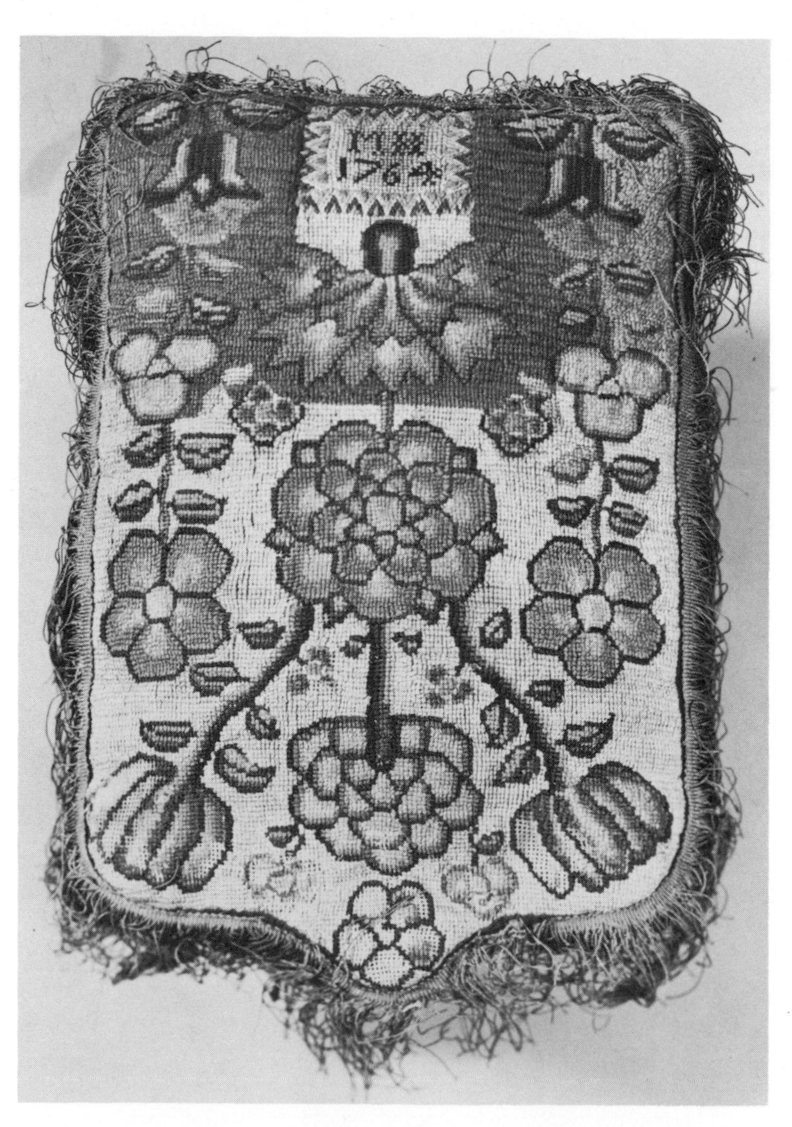

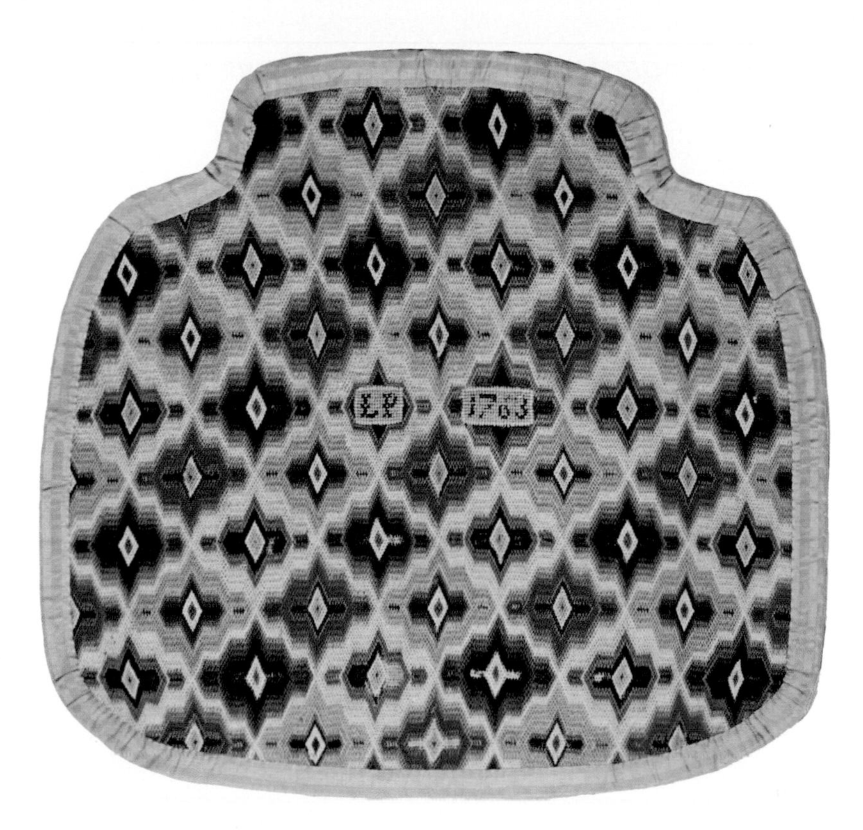

Seat cover initialed and dated "L P 1763" for Lydia Painter, of Chester County. Embroidered in Florentine stitch, in wool, on a canvas ground. 20″ × 19″. CHESTER COUNTY HISTORICAL SOCIETY.

Cushion worked by Ann Marsh who died in Chester County in 1796. Embroidered in silk and wool, on canvas, using cross and petit point stitches. 22″ × 17½″. CHESTER COUNTY HISTORICAL SOCIETY.

colours, Hat Sable. Clothed in Scarlet." He also mentions: "The School Mistris' Terms, and things to work with.

NEEDLES, of several sizes	Slave Silk	King Glass
CRUEL of all colours	Naples Silk	Gum Arabick
A TENT	Fine white alcomy wire	Gum Dragon

A SAMCLOTH, a cloth to sow on, a Canvice Cloth

The School Mistris' Terms of Art for all her ways of Sowing.

A Samcloth, vulgarly a Sampler.
Plat-Stitch or finger Plat Stitch, which is good on one side
Plat-Stitch or double Plat-Stitch, which is alike on both sides
Spanish stitch, true on both sides
Tent-stitch on the Finger
Tent-stitch on the Tent
Irish-stitch

Foze-stitch	Back-stitch
Gold-stitch	Queens-stitch
Tent-stitch upon Satin	Satin-stitch
Fern-stitch	Finny-stitch
New-stitch	Chain-stitch
Bead-stitch	Fishers-stitch
Rosemary-stitch	Dow-stitch
Whip-stitch	Cross-stitch
Raised Work	Needle work Pearl
Geneva Work	Virgins Device
Cut Work	Open Cut Work
Laid Work	Stitch-work & Through stitch
Lap Work	Rock Work
Frost Work	Nett work
Purle Work	Tent Work

Finger work, all which are several forts and manners of Works wrought by the Needle with Silk of all Natures, Purles, Wyres, &c. which cannot be described."

It is possible that the term "tent-stitch" was derived from the name of the early embroidery frame. Randle Holmes mentioned that the stitch could be worked in the hand, in a frame or upon satin.

Embroidery on a canvas ground is one of the strongest and most durable forms of needlework. Until the nineteenth century it was usual for the stitches to cover the entire ground, thereby strengthening the canvas made of either hemp, linen, flax, silk or gauze. The embroidery could be executed in wool, in silk, or in a combination of the two. Cross stitch or gros point and tent stitch or petit point are the two most frequently used stitches in canvas work.

Turkey work, which was an imitation of Oriental pile carpets, was used for upholstering furniture and for cushions in Pennsylvania. Wools were drawn through a canvas or coarse cloth foundation, knotted at the back and clipped at the front to form an even deep pile. In England it was popular during the Tudor period. Although no Pennsylvania examples of Turkey work are known to have survived it is not unusual to find mention of this type of needlework in the seventeenth and early eighteenth century inventories. An inventory, taken at the time of death, was an appraisal of a person's estate. William Wood, of Darby Township, in 1685 had "5 turkeworke cushons"; Ralph Fishbourn, of Chester, in 1708 had "½ doz of old Turks Work Chares"; James Sandeland, of Chester, in 1708 had "twenty four turkey work Chairs" and the inventory of Peter Boss, of Chichester Township, taken in 1708 lists a "peece of nedlework . . . 2 nedleworke Chaires & 1 Stoole . . . 1 Turkey work Back & Seate." The two needlework chairs could have been turkey work, crewel work, or needlework on a canvas ground. The inventory of Maurice Trent, mariner, of Chester County, taken in 1697 mentions "one table Carpet" which also could have been either turkey or canvas work. The listing of table carpets in Pennsylvania inventories is extremely rare.

In 1730 Martha Bulyn, of Kensington, worked a picture in petit point and background stitches.[1] In the center is a large tree

Pocket-book initialed and dated "G M 1765". Worked in wool, on canvas, in tent stitch. The colors used are rust, red, purple, yellow, blue and green. W. $6\frac{1}{2}$″, H. closed 5″, open $9\frac{1}{2}$″. MR. & MRS. SAMUEL W. MORRIS.

and birds. Under the tree standing on mounds is a shepherdess, deer, sheep, flowers and other animals. The combination of a shepherdess, sheep and a deer are found on samplers in the Philadelphia area be-

Portrait of George Washington. Worked in wool and silk, on canvas, using cross and petit point stitches. The colors used are red, purple, yellow, gray, brown, black, blue, green, white and pink. 35″ × 47½″. CHESTER COUNTY HISTORICAL SOCIETY.

ginning in the 1790's. Needlework pictures, to hang on the walls, had been popular in England.

The pincushion initialed and dated "M H 1764" for Martha Hickman of Chester County is wrought in both cross and petit point stitches. [p. 128] For the most part the ground is in cross stitch and the flowers and leaves in petit point. Around the edge there is a metallic thread fringe. The use of cross stitch for the ground is frequently employed as it adds strength to the finished article.

The man's pocket-book initialed and dated "G M 1765" is worked in petit point. [p. 131] The roses, tulips and carnations found on samplers, crewel and silk embroidery were also worked on canvas. Flowers are the motifs most frequently found in all types of needlework in Pennsylvania.

The chair seat decorated with flowers, leaves, shells and cornucopias was embroidered by Ann Marsh. The seat is worked in cross stitch for the ground, petit point for the flowers and leaves and French knots for the centers of the flowers. Silk threads were used as well as wool for contrasting texture. Ann Marsh did fine needlework. Silk pictures, [p. 99] a pincushion, [p. 99] a quilted petticoat,[2] a Florentine stitch cushion, [p. 124] a sampler[3] and this canvas work cushion are known to have been made by her before 1797 when she died in Chester County. [plate V]

From the latter part of the eighteenth century until about 1830 large portraits embroidered on a canvas ground were popular subjects for needlework. Many of the pictures were copied from prints, George Washington being the most usual subject. The large picture of Washington worked in wool and silk about 1820 is typical of its period. [p. 132] He stands in front of a background of draperies and columns. Behind him is a classical arm chair and in front of him is a draped classical table. Benjamin Franklin's portrait was also frequently executed on canvas. In later years sentimental and Biblical pictures take the place of the large portraits of American heroes.

BERLIN WORK

EMBROIDERY is a domestic form of art used by the women of all ages to enhance their homes and personal possessions. Needlework reflects the spirit of its age and until the craze for Berlin work developed in America in the mid-nineteenth century it was a means of individual expression for women.

During the period of the 1830's to the 1880's the craze for Berlin wool work virtually eclipsed all other types of embroidery. In fact in the minds of women the terms "embroidery" and "Berlin wool work" were regarded as synonymous. In 1847 the *Illuminated Book of Needlework* by Mrs. Henry Owen opens with the words: "Embroidery or as it is more often called Berlin wool-work" and later mentions that "This fashionable tapestry work, certainly the most useful kind of ornamental needlework, seems quite to have usurped the place of the various other embroideries which have, from time to time, engrossed the leisure moments of the fair. It may be called mechanical, and so in a degree it certainly is, but there is infinitely more scope for fancy, taste, and even genius here than in any other of the large family of satin stitches and embroideries.

"Yes, there is certainly room in worsted work for genius to exert itself—the genius of a painter in the selection and arrangement and combination of the colours and light and shade, etc. We do not mean in glaring arabesques, but in landscapes and portraits."[1]

By the 1840's Berlin wool work was almost as widespread in America as it was in England. The craze reached its height about 1856 and remained popular for the next thirty years.

Berlin wool work is a term generally applied to needlework, particularly that on a canvas ground, made during the Victorian era. According to the Countess of Wilton, Berlin wool work had its origin in the early nineteenth century when a print seller in Berlin, named Philipson, published the first colored designs on squared paper for needlework in 1804 or 1805.[2]

The first colored patterns upon paper were inferior in design and shading to those produced at a later time. In 1810 a print seller in Berlin, named Wittich, produced a series of these patterns which were copies of celebrated pictures. These were drawn upon "point paper" by good artists and cost £40 for the original. By 1840 there were at least 14,000 different patterns published. The designs were colored by hand on the squared paper so that the design could be copied onto square meshed canvas, each square of the design representing one stitch. Similar patterns were also published in France but in smaller quantities.

The pattern marked "Hertz & Wegener in Berlin Plate 1160" shows two dogs, bushes and flowers. [p. 136] On either side of the pattern are the same dogs worked on a double mesh canvas ground, using the suggested colors. The backgrounds have not been filled in.

Unfortunately few of the extant Berlin patterns are dated although they are generally numbered, presumably in sequence of publication. For this reason it is difficult to fix an exact date to a given pattern.

Mrs. Frances Trollope visited America in 1827 and 1828. When she returned to England she published a book, *Domestic Manners of the Americans*. In Philadelphia she noted that women went to societies to sew articles to be sold in bazaars:

Berlin pattern and pictures. Embroidered in wool, on canvas, using the tent stitch. The pattern is marked "Hertz & Wegener in Berlin Plate 1160". The colors used are red, brown, purple, green, gray, pink, lavender, orange, yellow, black and white. MORAVIAN MUSEUM OF BETHLEHEM.

She rises, and her first hour is spent in the scrupulously nice arrangement of her dress; she descends to her parlour neat, stiff, and silent; her breakfast is brought in by her free black footman; she eats her fried ham and her salt fish, and drinks her coffee in silence, while her husband reads one newspaper, and puts another under his elbow; and then, perhaps, she washes the cups and saucers. Her carriage is ordered at eleven; till that hour she is employed in the pastry-room, her snow-white apron protecting her mouse-coloured silk. Twenty minutes before her carriage should appear, she retires to her chamber, as she calls it, shakes, and folds up her still snow-white apron, smooths her rich dress, and with nice care, sets on her elegant bonnet, and all her handsome et caetera; then walks down stairs, just at the moment that her free black coachman announces to her free black footman that the carriage waits. She steps into it, and gives the word: "Drive to the Dorcas society." Her footman stays at home to clean the knives, but her coachman can trust his horses while he opens the carriage door, and his lady not being accustomed to a hand or an arm, gets out very safely without, though one of her own is occupied by a work-basket, and the other by a large roll of all those indescribable matters which ladies take as offerings to Dorcas societies. She enters the parlour appropriated for the meeting, and finds seven other ladies, very like herself, and takes her place among them; she presents her contribution, which is accepted with a gentle circular smile, and her parings of broad cloth, her ends of ribbon, her gilt paper, and her minikin pins, are added to the parings

> of broad cloth, the ends of ribbon, the gilt paper, and the minikin pins with which the table is already covered; she also produces from her basket three ready-made pincushions, four ink-wipers, seven paper matches, and a paste-board watch-case; these are welcomed with acclamations, and the youngest lady present deposits them carefully on shelves, amid a prodigious quantity of similar articles. She them produces her thimble, and asks for work; it is presented to her, and the eight ladies all stitch together for some hours.[3]

Elaborate pictorial designs, with religious, historical and romantic subjects were popular for framed pictures. Many of the needlework pictures were copies of popular pictures and prints of the period.

In 1850 Phebe Ann Sharpless, of Chester County, embroidered a romantic country scene including hunting dogs flushing a goose from a swamp. [below] In the background there are ducks on a pond and a Continental type house and mountains. The picture is wrought in wool on canvas, using cross and petit point stitches.

Picture by Phebe Ann Sharpless, of Chester County, worked in 1850. Embroidered in wool, on canvas, using cross and petit point stitches. The colors used are blue, red, white, purple, brown, yellow, gray, beige and black. 30″ × 22½″. CHESTER COUNTY HISTORICAL SOCIETY.

The true Berlin wool work was worked entirely in cross stitch or tent stitch in wools which were manufactured at Gotha and dyed in Berlin or in colored wools spun and dyed in England. The German wools were superior in texture and in the varieties of their dyes to the English wools. The worsted wools were called Zephyr yarns in Germany and Berlin wools in England, hence the name given to this type of needlework.

Various types of canvas for Berlin wool work were available, mostly imported from Germany, England and France. The Berlin silk canvas was the most expensive and was made in black, white or pearl gray. It was of a very fine mesh and needed no grounding. The German cotton canvas was the cheapest. Every tenth thread was yellow which facilitated counting the threads. The French canvas had a square even mesh and the English Penelope canvas was distinguished by the threads being in sets of four.

In America, in addition to the available Berlin patterns sold in the stores, there were women's monthly magazines that published instructions and patterns, sometimes in full color. *Godey's Lady's Book* was published in Philadelphia. It was America's most fashionable periodical and it did a great deal towards diffusing the cultural and moral ideas of the period. Many women considered it the ultimate authority in matters of culture and taste. *Petersen's Magazine* and *Leslie's Ladies' Gazette* also published instructions and patterns as did *Harper's Bazar* at a later date. The first volume of *Godey's Lady's Book* in 1830 mentions:

> . . . Patterns for working may be purchased at most of the fancy shops; but ladies possessing a taste for drawing may design their own subjects, by making sketches on paper, in pencil and afterwards going over them in ink. A pattern may be copied by placing a thin piece of paper over the original and tracing it through against a window. The outline of a subject already worked, if of a thick rich description may be obtained by laying the muslin on a table, placing a piece of white paper over it, and

> rubbing the paper with a nutmeg; this outline may afterwards, be perfected with a pen.[4]

The following year the magazine stated:

> Paper patterns, covered with black cross lines, to represent threads of canvas, and painted on the squares in the proper colours, may be bought at the worsted-shops; but in working from these patterns, it is necessary to use the cross-stitch, which is taken in an angular direction over two threads of the canvas, and then crossed in the same manner. The pattern is not to be tacked to the canvas, but merely placed in view, as a copy. The center of the middle flower, or ornament, is to be first ascertained, and the coloured squares in the pattern counted from it, as a guide for the number of stitches to be taken in each colour on the canvas.[5]

Religious pictures, particularly subjects from the Old Testament, were popular subjects for needlework. Some are signed and dated. The picture "Suffer Little Children to come unto Me" is wrought in cross stitch on canvas about 1825. [p. 116] Another Scriptural picture is signed "Amanda Elizabeth Arnolds Work 1856."[6] It is wrought on canvas, using cross stitch and double cross stitch. Three religious figures sit in front of a romantic background. A child is sitting on a woman's lap and there are doves, squirrels, many flowers and perhaps the girl's own dog. In the absence of documentation such as a name and date, it is difficult to assign an exact date to these embroidered pictures. The majority of the Biblical pictures were copied from contemporary paintings. Size meant nothing. When paintings were large embroideries were also large. Needlework painting remained in style until the 1880's.

The cross stitch picture marked "Catharine Calls Work 1854" shows three maidens in a rural setting. [p. 141] In the foreground is a pet dog and two dolls and in the background trees, bushes and a dove. This picture is unusual as the faces and hands have not been executed in petit point stitch.

Petersen's Magazine, in February of 1844 mentions that

> Figures in embroidery usually have the best effect when worked in wool and silk, with a judicious mixture of gold and silver beads. The hair and drapery should be worked in cross-stitch, and the face, neck and hands, in tent-stitch; work four of the latter for one of the former. Nearly the whole beauty of the work will depend on obtaining proper tints for the face . . . Next to the face, the drapery requires the most care and skill . . .

Miss Lambert in the *Hand-book of Needlework* mentions that

> Needlework may be regarded (if we may be allowed the expression) as the sister art of painting; the aim of the accomplished needlewoman of the present day, being to produce as true a picture of nature as possible; soaring far beyond the common-place ideas of the ancient embroideries, which perhaps, are more to be admired for the richness of their materials, and the labour bestowed upon them, than for any merit they possess as works of art . . .[7]

Floral designs were the most popular, particularly for upholstery and smaller domestic articles such as hand screens, reticules, bags, purses, pincushions, pillows, needlebooks, album covers, blotters and all sorts of knick-knacks for the home. Wreaths of flowers and bouquets were worked in vivid colors with dazzling effect, for aniline dyes had been invented, which surpassed in harsh brilliancy the hues obtained by vegetable dyes. The peacock greens and blues, magentas, violets and pinks were used with more enthusiasm than discrimination. In the 1830's and 1840's the floral wreaths and bouquets usually had a light color background. In the 1850's a black or dark color background became more usual. This served to emphasize the harsh, garish colors of the Berlin wools. Birds, particularly parrots in Pennsylvania, were often introduced into the designs. The popularity of bird patterns in Berlin work may have been inspired by the magnificent bird books published at this time. Audubon's *Birds of America* was widely circulated in England and America, but more influential were the *Birds of Australia* and the *Monograph of the Ramphastidae or Family of Toucans* by John Gould and the *Illustrations of the Family of Psittacidae or Parrotts* by Edward Lear. Some of the Berlin patterns were copied directly from these books. The exotic birds, usually parrots or macaws, were eminently suited for raised Berlin wool work.

Pictures, fire screens and cushions frequently had designs that incorporated birds in brilliant plumage and flowers. The cushion having a parrot, roses and a lily was embroidered in wool and beads. [p. 143] The bird is wrought in plush stitch in a series of loops

Picture inscribed "Catharine Calls Work 1854". Embroidered in wool, on canvas, using cross stitch. The colors used are green, blue, pink, red, brown, tan, orange, gray, black and white. 33″ × 26″. HISTORICAL SOCIETY OF BERKS COUNTY.

which were afterwards cut to give the effect of a thick velvet pile raised above the foundation. The shearing of the wool was graduated to emphasize the form of the bird and to give it a three-dimensional, realistic effect. The bird's eye is a large bead. The roses, lily and other flowers are worked in the plush stitch. The leaves and branches are formed of beads.

A variety of Berlin work known as German embroidery in which beads, silk and chenille thread were introduced into the designs were used on pillows, chair seats, pincushions and other accessories. As the Victorian era developed, ornamentation and beauty became synonymous terms.

Pet dogs and cats were frequently depicted in needlework. Raised Berlin wool work was popular for animals as well as birds and flowers. Wreaths of flowers against either a light or a dark background were extremely colorful and popular. Frequently they were wrought in raised Berlin wool work as cushions or to be framed and hung on the wall.

The Young Ladies' Treasure Book was full of ideas for increasing the ornamental contents of each room. In the chapter on "Taste and Care of the Household" it mentions that, "Girls who are clever with their fingers can do much towards making the home beautiful, not only by needlework, painting, drawing, and the various kinds of fancywork, but by the practice of amateur upholstery . . ."[8]

The Victorians had a desire to cram and decorate their rooms. Underfoot there might be a floral carpet and large figured wallpaper all around; there are overstuffed chairs, tufted ottomans, marble-topped tables, carved sideboards and pianos; the remaining space is garnished with potted plants, bronze statuary, plaster casts, wax flowers under glass domes, shellwork, beadwork, hair mementos, feather wreaths, fringed cushions, gilt-framed pictures and petit point mottoes; souvenirs and bric-a-brac are arranged on fretwork brackets and tiered whatnots.

Berlin patterns were also executed on wool, satin or other

1857 picture by Mary S. Yackel. Embroidered in wool, on canvas, using cross stitch. The colors used are red, blue, pink, brown, orange, yellow, gray, black and white. 27″ × 26″. SCHWENKFELDER LIBRARY.

Pillow. Embroidered in wool and beads, on canvas, using flat and plush stitches. The colors of wool used are yellow, brown, purple, green, tan, red and white. 18″ × 18″. LANCASTER COUNTY HISTORICAL SOCIETY.

materials by stitching a canvas over the material. The design was worked by counting the squares and the stitches were taken through both the canvas and the ground material. When the design was completed the canvas threads were withdrawn leaving the needlework on the intended material. The handbooks of the period mention that a large picture should be started at the bottom and that when grounding one should begin at the lower left-hand corner.

Miss Lambert mentions that "Berlin patterns have contributed more towards the advancement of needlework of the present day, than any improvement that has of late years been introduced into the art,—not simply from the assistance they yield the needlewoman, but from the demand they have occasioned for improved and superior materials . . ."[9]

The picture worked by Mary S. Yackel, in 1857, has in the center a bird perched on a spray of roses, and a spandrel of roses and leaves in each corner. [p. 143] During the Victorian era the cabbage-like rose was one of the most popular motifs. It is also found on furniture, silver, rugs, et cetera, of the period. The picture was wrought on a fine canvas which needed no grounding. The use of many bright colors in one picture is also typical of Victorian needlework.

Phebe Kriebel, a girl of German descent, who lived in Towamencin Township, Montgomery County, embroidered a picture which she signed and dated in 1857. [plate VI] At this time she was twenty years old. The lively charming picture is amusingly out of scale with roses in the background larger than the trains, boats, human figures, et cetera, in the foreground. The scene is one of great activity. There are many houses, churches, horses with carts and wagons, a stage coach, trains and both sail and steam boats. There are also many different varieties of trees, animals and birds depicted in wool and silk on the canvas ground, using gobelin, petit point and satin stitches. Other similar pictures are known to have been made in Pennsylvania.

1857 picture worked by Phebe Kriebel. Embroidered in wool, on canvas, using gobelin, petit point and satin stitches. 27″ × 25″. SCHWENKFELDER MUSEUM.

Berlin wool work was used for needlework rugs, carriage rugs and carpets. A thick wool and a coarse canvas was usually employed.

Many of the smaller Berlin patterns were worked in wool or silk on perforated card or Bristol board. Mottoes such as "God Bless Our Home," "Home Sweet Home," "In God We Trust" and "God Bless Our Union" were popular to frame and hang on the walls. Book markers mounted on ribbon, greeting cards, portfolios, pictures, samplers, needlebooks, watch holders and baskets are among the articles made.

This was a time when women moralized on every possible occasion. The ladies set great store by their accomplishments and an interminable amount of time went into the making of elegant knick-knacks for the home.

LEFT. Victorian side chair. Embroidered in crepe and silk, on satin, using French knot and satin stitches. The colors used are red, blue, yellow, pink and green. ANNIE S. KEMERER MUSEUM.

RIGHT. Victorian side chair. The back and seat embroidered in wool, on canvas, using gobelin and petit point stitches. The colors used are blue, red, pink, green, yellow, and black. ANNIE S. KEMERER MUSEUM.

During the nineteenth century needlepoint and cross stitch were frequently used for the coverings of chairs, sofas, benches, piano and foot stools. Floral, ornamental and geometric patterns were extremely popular. More unusual is the Victorian side chair having floral motifs, dragons and romantic scenes on the back and seat. [p. 145] The ground was worked in black wool, using the gobelin stitch. The scenes are well executed in petit point stitch. Maidens, young men and ruins of classical buildings against a romantic landscape were favorite motifs of the Victorian embroideress.

Table cloth. Embroidered in wool and metallic thread using satin, buttonhole and clipped wool-work. The plates and parts of the knives and forks are cotton appliqué. The colors used are green, yellow, lavender, purple, pink, red and white on a black background. SCHWENKFELDER MUSEUM.

A chair seat having a spray of flowers in the center and a scroll, vines and flowers around the border was worked in green, gray and black wool in cross stitch.[10] Half of the center leaves, the scroll, circles and centers of the flowers are made of cut steel, crystal, gold and white beads. Geometric and diaper patterns, Greek key borders, folded ribbons, scrolls and arabesques and vine leaves with perhaps a small flower here and there gained in popularity.

A particularly interesting Victorian chair is one having the round back and seat embroidered in crepe and silk, on vivid blue satin, using French knot and satin stitches. [p. 145] The flowers and leaves are in brilliant shades of red, blue, yellow, pink and green. Petal by petal the flowers have been built up and attached to the satin ground, giving the embroidery a realistic three-dimensional effect. This type of embroidery was generally wrought on pictures [p. 110] and only rarely employed for upholstery.

The round black table cloth, with place settings, fruit and vegetables is a unique piece of Victorian needlework. [p. 146] The white cotton plates and platter and the gray knife and forks are appliquéd on the cloth. The plates and platter have a purple border and the flowers are embroidered with satin and buttonhole stitches in pink, red, yellow, lavender and green wool. The butter plates are white silk outlined with a metal thread. The grapes, apple, pear, peach, squash, carrot, lemon, cucumber and knife and fork handles are worked in plush stitch. The fruit and vegetables stand up from the platter about one and a half inches.

Berlin work had a very wide appeal. It was an almost mechanical art where an ability to count and time to embroider was all that was needed. Skill with the needle was not necessary.

At the Philadelphia Centennial Exhibition in 1876 The Royal School of Art Needlework's exhibit brought about the revival of embroidery as a fine art in America. Berlin wool work gave way to "art needlework."

PENNSYLVANIA GERMAN NEEDLEWORK

NEXT to the settlers from the British Isles, the largest national group coming to Pennsylvania during the Colonial period were the Germans who migrated chiefly from the Upper Rhine Valley. William Penn, knowing of their political discontent, religious persecution and hard times, had sent agents to Europe to encourage families from the Palatine, the Upper Rhine, Swabia and Switzerland to migrate to Pennsylvania.

The Pennsylvania Germans, sometimes called Pennsylvania Dutch, faithfully perpetuated their European customs. This was made possible because the settlers arrived in Pennsylvania in an almost continuous stream between 1683 and 1775 and settled in a closely confined area. As a result, even daily contact with other language groups failed to weaken their European traditions.

Leaving villages in which native crafts flourished they transplanted the traditional peasant style of the Old World to the New. The early settlers were simple folk, farmers for the most part. Sentiment, love of nature and symbolism were important in the lives of these men and women.

The Pennsylvania German needlework found especially on

samplers and show towels is pleasantly decorative and colorful. They had a desire to add gaiety to life by decorating everyday utilitarian articles.

During the nineteenth century, when flax culture was at its height, much needlework was done by the Pennsylvania Germans. Samplers were usually embroidered by the children and show towels, bed and table linen by the older women. Most of the needlework was embroidered on homespun in cross stitch, using either cotton or linen thread. As the century progressed bright wools and a few of the more elaborate stitches were used.

The custom of covering the guest towel that hung on a rack on the door with an ornately decorated show towel, called in German, *Paradenhandtücher,* was common in both Germany and in Pennsylvania. To the Pennsylvania German housewife the show towel was a symbol of cleanliness and prosperity as well as being a means of decorating the home. The surviving Pennsylvania show towels are similar to European ones. The same motifs used in Europe were also employed in Pennsylvania. Before 1820 dated show towels are extremely rare. Those known are longer and thinner than those bearing a later date. The early show towels are worked in cotton on homespun. A few of the later examples are embroidered on a background having a woven design. Like samplers, many of the show towels have initials and dates.

The drawn work show towel dated 1807 includes a pair of birds, zigzag lines and at the bottom simple Tree of Life motifs. [p. 151] It is embroidered entirely in white. Drawn work is frequently encountered on show towels. It is of a delicate lace-like nature, necessitating the removal of certain weft or warp threads of the material and adding decorative stitchery upon those which remain. Sometimes the stitchery was worked with colored thread.

The show towel initialed and dated "1816 A G" is unusual as it is embroidered in wool and silk on linen, using stem, chain and cross stitches. [p. 152] The pairs of birds, waving lines and Tree of Life motifs are worked in gold, red, blue, pink and green.

The show towel dated 1827 is embroidered in linen on cotton entirely in cross stitch in shades or red, yellow, tan, blue, pink, green and black. [p. 151] Included in the design are simple transverse borders of embroidery and fringe. Extremely rare is the star design on the Tree of Life and the two angels holding the garland. The garland is an old Pagan ornament that represents the joy of Nature and the rejoicing of the fruitful earth. The stars, baskets of fruit, pairs of birds, hearts and crown motifs were motifs used on many Pennsylvania samplers.

The show towel initialed and dated "L C Z 1837" is embroidered in pink throughout. [p. 151] The towel includes both cross stitch and drawn work.

In 1841 Mary Nissly embroidered a cotton show towel in cross stitch. [p. 151] At the top she worked her name and two stars. Beneath that she embroidered a crowned heart from which six lilies grow interspersed with the initials O E H B D D E, these being the first letters of the words "O Edles Herz Bedenk Dach Dein Ende" (O Noble Heart Reflect on your End). The mentioning of where she lived is unusual:

> Mary Nissly is my name Rapho is my Station Heaven
> is my dwelling place and Christ is my Salvation when I am
> dead and in my Grave and all my bones are rotten when
> This you see remember me for Else I Shall be Forgotten
> Rapho Township Lancaster County and State of Pennsylvania
> I markd this handtoul January the 2 1841

The design includes a table and two chairs, two prancing deer under a tree, two large peacocks, stars, Tree of Life motifs and simple cross borders. At the bottom she worked a small amount of drawn work and a fringe.

LEFT.
1841 show towel by Mary Nissly, of Lancaster County. Embroidered in cotton on linen using cross stitch. The colors used are red, blue and black. 16″ × 68″.
MARY ANN MCILNAY.

RIGHT.
1827 show towel. Embroidered in cotton on linen using cross stitch. The colors used are red, yellow, tan, blue, pink, green and black. 16″ × 66″.
MARY ANN MCILNAY.

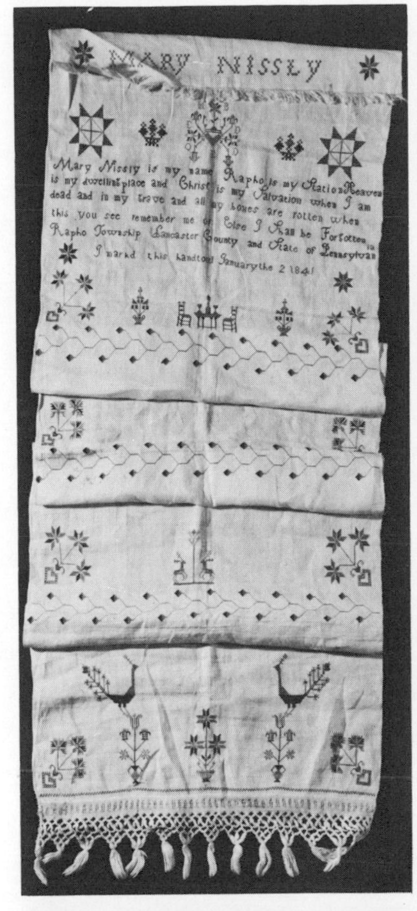

LEFT.
1807 Drawn work show towel. 64″ × 17½″.
MARY ANN MCILNAY.

RIGHT.
1837 show towel marked "L C Z". Embroidered in pink cotton on linen using cross stitch. 15″ × 68″.
JOE KINDIG, JR.

The table cloth dated 1795 is worked in cotton on fine linen using cross stitch in shades of red, pink and black. [p. 153] Nineteenth century Pennsylvania German table cloths are frequently square and include scattered motifs and sometimes names, dates, alphabets and sentiments.

The pillow case initialed and dated "A L M 1824" is worked in cotton on fine linen in cross stitch. [p. 153] Both Pennsylvania Germans and the women of English descent frequently initialed and less often both initialed and dated their household linens.

The needlecase is embroidered in wool on a linen ground using satin, cross, bullion knot and couching stitches. [below] The outside of the case is chintz. The motifs used are similar to those found on samplers and show towels. Since the needlecase is embroidered in wool on linen it is an excellent example of Pennsylvania German crewel work.

LEFT. Needlecase. Embroidered in wool on a linen background. The outside of the needlecase is chintz. The stitches used are satin, cross, buttonhole, bullion knots and couching. The colors used are yellow, gold, red, blue and brown. 21″ × $4\frac{3}{4}$″. MARY ANN McILNAY.

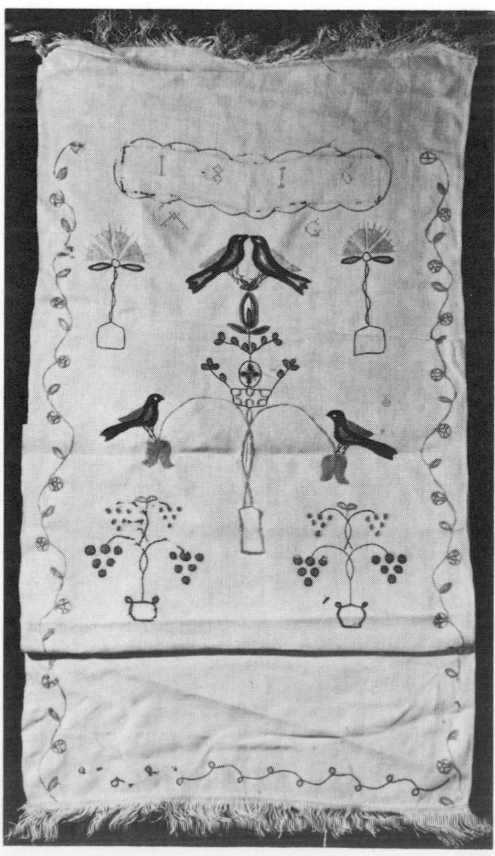

1816 show towel marked "A G". Embroidered in wool and silk on linen using stem, chain and cross stitches. The colors used are gold, red, blue, pink and green. 54″ × $17\frac{1}{2}$″. MARY ANN McILNAY.

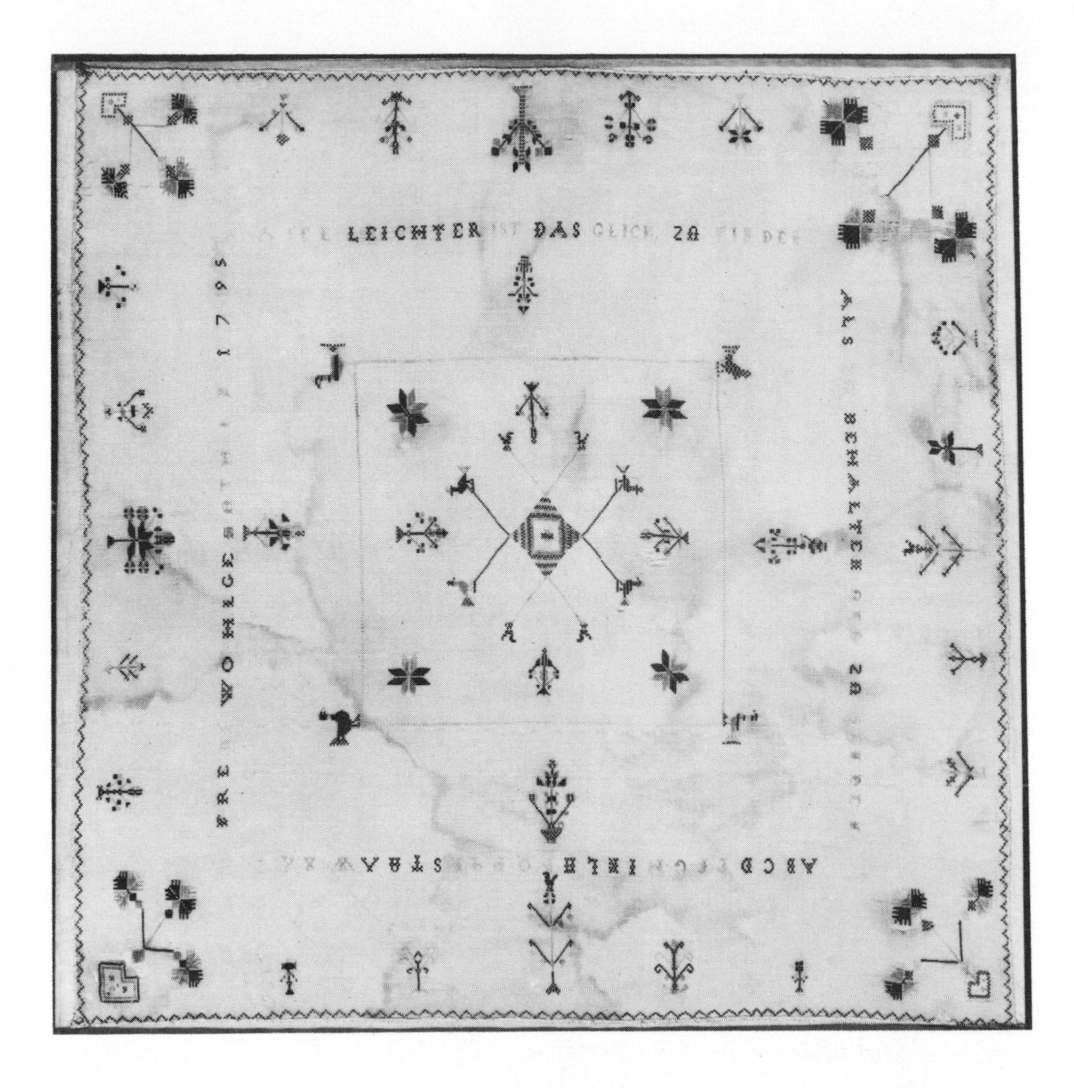

1795 table cloth. Embroidered in cotton on linen using cross stitch. The colors used are red, pink and black. 21″ × 21″. MARY ANN McILNAY.

1824 pillow case. Embroidered in cotton on linen using cross stitch. The colors used are red, tan and black. 32″ × 17″. MARY ANN McILNAY.

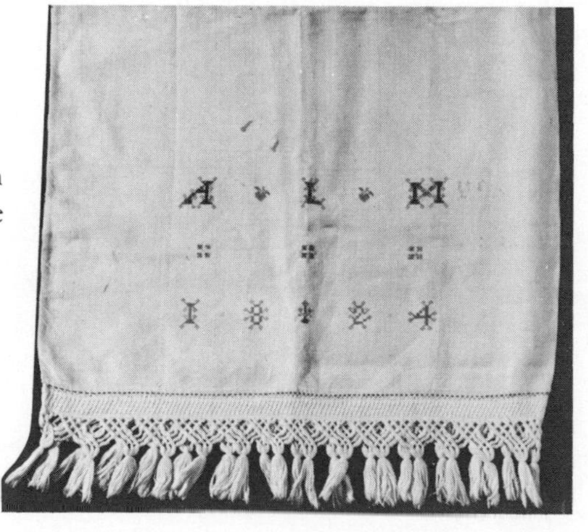

STUMP WORK

STUMP work or embroidery on the stamp is a style of needlework which was popular in England during the reign of James I, remaining popular through the Commonwealth and the reign of Charles II—that would be roughly 1625 to 1700. It is uncertain as to whether stump work was of German origin or introduced by the nuns of Little Gidding, in England. The obvious characteristic of stump work is the high relief produced by padding and stuffing in many parts of the design. The designs were directly drawn or traced, possibly from Natural History, Botany or Emblem books, onto the satin, silk or canvas ground. White satin was the most common. The flat details were then embroidered directly on the background material. The raised figures were constructed separately, padded with wool, cotton or hair and when completed they were backed with paper to prevent the edges from fraying and sewn, usually with the buttonhole stitch, to the ground.

Many of the stumped figures may almost be regarded as dolls with beautiful costumes and accessories worked in minute detail. Heads, hands and legs were sometimes carved from wood and either covered with buttonhole stitch or else painted. Faces, if wood, could be covered with white satin, the features being either embroidered in silk or painted. The faces, if not stumped, were worked in split stitch on the ground. The women liked the conceit of hands, leaves and flower petals attached at one end so as to stand free, doors half open and windows with isinglass to give an illusion of depth. Animals, birds, butterflies, fruits and flowers were used to fill every space and there was a general disregard for proportion and perspective. Brillant colors, the use of seed pearls, sequins, gold and silver thread, colored purl, which was wire coiled spring fashion and sometimes covered with silk, beads as well as the use of rich textiles, feathers and lace give stump work an exotic appearance. The favorite subjects were generally taken from the Old Testament, the Royal house of Stuart, or are symbolic groups placed on an English landscape. Kings and Queens, castles, houses, tents, mounds, rockeries, wells, fountains and fishponds were also popular subjects. Embroidery on the stamp was used to decorate caskets, boxes of all sizes, looking glass frames and was embroidered as pictures. Infinite trouble and ingenuity were exercised in stump work.

Seventeenth century American examples of stump work are extremely rare. In Pennsylvania there are no known examples. Few women had the time, experience or materials to execute such an elaborate piece of needlework.

In the mid-nineteenth century there was a small revival of interest in stump work. Anna Lippincott, born in 1848 in East Bradford Township, Chester County, embroidered a picture of a man and woman standing under a bower. The faces are unfinished, they have been drawn in pencil on the satin ground. Overhead there are rain clouds while the sun shines. A parrot is perched between the people and there are also a peacock, lion, turkey, caterpillar, insects and scattered flowers. The wings of the insects and a few of the leaves are attached to the satin at one end, standing free at the other. Much of the embroidery is wrought directly on the ground in silk. Anna Lippincott also used a lot of gimp and metallic threads. The faces and clothes of the man and woman are in the Stuart tradition as is the inclusion of over-scaled insects, lions, peacocks and the sun and rain clouds in the sky at the same time. The treatment of the trees is purely Victorian. [p. 156]

This picture worked in the nineteenth century is not as well designed or executed as known seventeenth century English examples of embroidery on the stamp. Anna Lippincott's picture is the only Pennsylvania stump work picture that has been found. Few women during this period, when the craze for Berlin work was at its height, seem to have had the ability, the interest, or been willing to take the time necessary to execute this elaborate type of needlework. Berlin work, simpler and quicker to work, was popular until the introduction of "art needlework" in America in 1876. English teachers of needlework came to America to teach the women to make copies of the fine Elizabethan and Queen Anne embroideries. At this time Decorative Art Societies were organized in New York, Philadelphia, Boston and Chicago, concerned with the revival of embroidery as an art in America.

Stump work picture by Anna Lippincott who was born in Chester County in 1848. Worked with gimp, silk and metal threads and materials. The colors used are blue, tan, yellow, brown, black, gold, green, white and red. 22″ × 15½″. CHESTER COUNTY HISTORICAL SOCIETY.

NOTES

SAMPLERS

1. Ethel Stanwood Bolton and Eva Johnston Coe, *American Samplers,* (Massachusetts Society of the Colonial Dames of America, 1921), p. 67.
2. George N. Highley Collection.
3. Titus C. Geesey Collection.
4. *American Weekly Mercury,* (Phila., Pa.) March 5, 1728.
5. Thomas Woody, *Early Quaker Education in Pennsylvania,* (Teachers College, Columbia University, N.Y.C.), p. 191.
6. Woody, op. cit., p. 192.
7. Woody, op. cit., p. 215.
8. Mr. & Mrs. Medford J. Brown Collection.
9. Bolton and Coe, op. cit., p. 84.
10. W. T. Ashbridge, *The Ashbridge Book Relating To Past and Present Ashbridge Families in America,* (Toronto, Canada), p. 118.
11. Bolton and Coe, op. cit., p. 42.
12. Franklin Ellis and Samuel Evans, *History of Lancaster County, Pennsylvania,* (Phila., 1883), p. 404.
13. *Lancaster Journal,* (Lancaster, Penna.), April 21, 1797.
14. Ibid., Oct. 19, 1799.
15. Cooper Union Museum Collection.
16. Bolton and Coe, op. cit., Plate XLVIII.
17. Cooper Union Museum Collection.
18. Watson W. and Sarah B. Dewees, *History of Westtown Boarding School* 1799–1899 (Phila., Penna.), p. 45.
19. Helen G. Hole, *Westtown through the Years* 1799–1942, (Westtown, Penna., 1942) p. 56.
21. Mary Ann Mc Ilnay Collection.
22. Chester County Historical Society.
23. Bolton and Coe, op. cit., Plate XCVI.
24. Henry Francis duPont Winterthur Museum Collection.
25. Bolton and Coe, op. cit., p. 172.
26. Dewees, op. cit., p. 56.
27. Morton L. Montgomery, *Historical and Biographical Annals of Berks County Pennsylvania,* (Chicago, Ill., 1909), p. 365.
28. *Pennsylvania Magazine of History and Biography,* (Historical Society of Pennsylvania, Phila.), Vol. 24, p. 125.
29. Radnor Historical Society Collection.
30. Chester County Historical Society Collection.
31. *American Republican,* (West Chester, Penna.), June 20, 1815.
32. *Village Record,* (West Chester, Penna.), Feb. 3, 1819.
33. Mercer Museum of Bucks County Historical Society Collection.
34. Chester County Historical Society Collection.
35. Bolton and Coe, op. cit., p. 172.
36. Chester County Historical Society Collection.
37. *Chester and Delaware Federalist,* (West Chester, Penna.), June 17, 1812.
38. Ellis and Evans, op. cit., p.
39. *Aurora General Advertiser,* (Phila., Penna.), Jan. 1, 1818.
40. Bolton and Coe, op. cit., Plate XCVI.
41. Bolton and Coe, op. cit., Plate XCVI.
42. Cooper Union Museum Collection.
43. Bolton and Coe, op. cit., p. 186.
44. Historical Society of Pennsylvania Collection.
45. Bolton and Coe, op. cit., p. 140.
46. Mr. and Mrs. Alfred Clegg Collection.
47. Chester County Historical Society Collection.
48. Chester County Historical Society Collection.
49. Luther C. Parsons, *The Lower Merion Academy,* (Historical Society of Montgomery County, 1915), p. 147.
50. Bolton and Coe, op. cit., p. 198.
51. Bolton and Coe, op. cit., p. 187.
52. Bolton and Coe, op. cit., Plate LXXIII.
53. Bolton and Coe, op. cit., p. 144.

54. Bolton and Coe, op. cit., p. 199.
55. Bolton and Coe, op. cit., p. 221.
56. *American Republican,* (West Chester, Penna.), Jan. 22, 1827.
57. Ibid., Aug. 27, 1827.
58. *Village Record,* (West Chester, Penna.), April 21, 1830.
59. Ibid., May 12, 1830.
60. Ibid., April 25, 1832.
61. Ibid., April 30, 1834.
62. Ibid., June 4, 1834.
63. Ibid., March 26, 1839.
64. Ibid., May 29, 1849.
65. Cooper Union Museum.

CREWEL EMBROIDERY

1. Delaware County Historical Society
2. Mrs. Harold O. Ladd

SILK EMBROIDERY

1. Stevenson W. Fletcher, *Pennsylvania Agriculture and Country Life,* (Harrisburg, 1850), p. 2.
2. Fletcher, op. cit., p. 3.
3. *Pennsylvania Journal or Weekly Advertiser,* (Philadelphia, Penna.), Aug. 17, 1749. Phoebe P. Prime Files, Winterthur Museum Libraries.
4. *Pennsylvania Journal,* (Philadelphia, Penna.), May 26, 1768. Phoebe P. Prime Files, Winterthur Museum Libraries.
5. *Pennsylvania Packet,* (Philadelphia, Penna.), Jan. 30, 1775. Phoebe P. Prime Files, Winterthur Museum Libraries.
6. *Pennsylvania Packet,* (Philadelphia, Penna.), Sept. 2, 1790. Phoebe P. Prime Files, Winterthur Museum Libraries.
7. *Federal Gazette,* (Philadelphia, Penna.), March 5, 1793. Phoebe P. Prime Files, Winterthur Museum Libraries.

MORAVIAN NEEDLEWORK

1. William C. Reichel and William H. Bigler, *A History of the Moravian Seminary for Young Ladies at Bethlehem, Pennsylvania,* (Bethlehem, Penna., 1901), p. 26.
2. Mabel Haller, *Early Moravian Education in Pennsylvania,* p. 17.
3. Maryland Historical Society Collection.
4. Reichel and Bigler, op. cit., p. 51.
5. Reichel and Bigler, op. cit., p. 168.
6. Reichel and Bigler, op. cit., p. 79.
7. Reichel and Bigler, op. cit., p. 79.
8. Reichel and Bigler, op. cit., p. 111.
9. Reichel and Bigler, op. cit., p. 84.
10. Reichel and Bigler, op. cit., p. 200.
11. Reichel and Bigler, op. cit., p. 222.
12. Reichel and Bigler, op. cit., p. 207.
13. Reichel and Bigler, op. cit., p. 24.
14. *A Century and Three Quarters of Life and Service,* (Linden Hall Seminary, Lititz, Penna.), p. 10.
15. Ibid., p. 9.
16. Linden Hall School Collection.
17. Linden Hall School Collection.

FLORENTINE STITCH EMBROIDERY

1. *Antiques Magazine,* June 1931, p. 476.

CANVAS WORK

1. Ethel Stanwood Bolton and Eva Johnston Coe, *American Samplers,* (Massachusetts Society of the Colonial Dames of America, 1921), p. 35.
2. Chester County Historical Society Collection.
3. George N. Highley Collection.

BERLIN WORK

1. Mrs. Henry Owen, *The Illuminated Book of Needlework.* Edited by the Countess of Wilton (London, 1847).
2. Countess of Wilton, *The Art of Needlework,* (London 1840).
3. Frances Trollope, *Domestic Manners of the Americans,* (New York, 1927), p. 240, 241.
4. *Godey's Lady's Book,* Vol. 1, p. 3.
5. *Godey's Ladies' Magazine,* Jan. 1831, p. 26.
6. Berks County Historical Society.
7. Miss Lambert, *Hand-book of Needlework,* (New York, 1842), p. 14.
8. *The Young Ladies' Treasure Book,* (London, n.d.), p. 195.
9. Lambert, op. cit., p. 76.
10. Moravian Museum of Bethlehem.

INDEX

Numbers in bold face refer to illustrations